The Puppy That Came for Christmas

How a Dog Brought One Family the Gift of Joy

MEGAN RIX

A PLUME BOOK

PLUME
Published by the Penguin Group
Penguin Group (USA) Inc., 375 Hudson Street, New York, New York 10014, U.S.A. •
Penguin Group (Canada), 90 Eglinton Avenue East, Suite 700, Toronto, Ontario,
Canada M4P 2Y3 (a division of Pearson Penguin Canada Inc.) • Penguin Books Ltd.,
80 Strand, London WC2R 0RL, England • Penguin Ireland, 25 St. Stephen's Green,
Dublin 2, Ireland (a division of Penguin Books Ltd.) • Penguin Group (Australia),
250 Camberwell Road, Camberwell, Victoria 3124, Australia (a division of Pearson
Australia Group Pty. Ltd.) • Penguin Books India Pvt. Ltd., 11 Community Centre,
Panchsheel Park, New Delhi – 110 017, India • Penguin Group (NZ), 67 Apollo
Drive, Rosedale, Auckland 0632, New Zealand (a division of Pearson New Zealand
Ltd.) • Penguin Books (South Africa) (Pty.) Ltd., 24 Sturdee Avenue, Rosebank,
Johannesburg 2196, South Africa

Penguin Books Ltd., Registered Offices: 80 Strand, London WC2R 0RL, England

Published by Plume, a member of Penguin Group (USA) Inc. Previously published
in Great Britain by Penguin Books Ltd.

First Plume Printing, November 2011
10 9 8 7 6 5 4 3

*Penguin is committed to publishing works of quality and integrity.
In that spirit, we are proud to offer this book to our readers;
however, the story, the experiences, and the words
are the author's alone.*

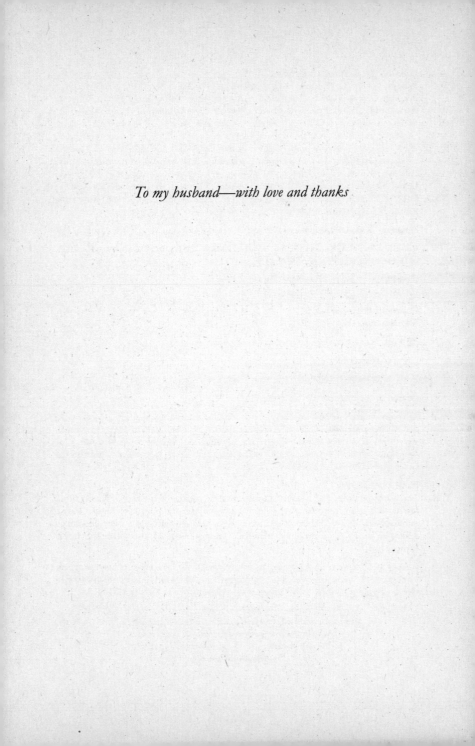

To my husband—with love and thanks

I

I crouched down beside the traveling crate and watched the two beautiful creamy-colored golden-retriever/Labrador-cross puppies snuggled up together, nose to tail in a ball, fast asleep. Six-and-a-half weeks old, just left Mum, and in a few moments I'd be taking one of them home.

Three months before, I'd never even thought about having a dog. But then, two years ago, I hadn't imagined I'd meet Ian that May, get engaged in Paris on his birthday (in August), and married on Waikiki Beach on my birthday (the following March). Two years ago, I was a determinedly single woman who hadn't thought much about fertility treatment or IVF, although at forty-three perhaps it was inevitable I'd have to if I wanted children. But it had all happened, and now here I was: about to take a new puppy life into my hands. Was I ready for this?

"Of course you are—or at least you'll have to be," I'd murmured as I looked myself in the eyes in the mirror, grabbed the car keys and hurried out of the door, heart thumping, to go and pick the puppy up.

As I looked down at the puppies, I had no idea that, however unprepared Ian and I were for the joys, challenges and downright disruptions of puppy parent life, it would be nothing compared with how unprepared we'd be to relinquish our beloved puppy when she passed on to the next stage of her training to become a Helper Dog for disabled people. The sun streamed into the crate and shone on the little dogs' fur. One of them whimpered; its back leg jerked, it gave itself a little scratch, and settled down again, asleep all the while. I had never seen anything so beautiful or so vulnerable.

"So sweet," I whispered.

Jamie, who ran the Helper Dogs center, nodded and whispered back in his gentle Scottish burr: "Yours is the little girl at the back. What do you think of the name Emma for her?"

"Emma," I repeated. "Lovely." Any name at all, in fact, would be lovely.

I took a deep breath and reached down to pick up the tiny warm bundle . . .

Before we were married, Ian was my best friend and always able to make me laugh—although considering we met on a stand-up comedy course that was hardly surprising. In fact, it was only luck that we ended up on the course at the same time. I should have started earlier, but I'd been asked to do some research and writing overseas, and had written three children's books in three different countries. Ian, though usually far more punctual than me, had also failed to attend the course at his first attempt due to overload at work, at a bank in the city. As part of our homework, the tutor told us to go out to comedy shows, to sensitize our ears to how to deliver a joke. I didn't like the idea of late-night gigs and the last tube home, so I arranged a class trip on a Sunday afternoon to see some stand-up in North London. I got terribly lost on the way and turned up late, all of a fluster. The pub was almost empty, voices and footsteps descending to the venue below, but there Ian was, the only one who had waited, obviously delighted to see me and not at all in a panic. He bought me a drink and we went downstairs.

After the show, Ian and I were left to talk together. His Stockport accent reminded me of good times spent as a student in Manchester, and we found we'd both worked with people with severe learning difficulties. Our friends seemed to melt away and time slipped by until we, alone now, decided to go to another comedy club up the road. Ian offered to drive us in his car. I thought he said he had a Jeep, so I was surprised when he held the passenger door open on a brand-new convertible BMW. He'd actually been trying to say he had GPS navigation, to reassure me we wouldn't get lost, and I'd misheard in the hubbub of the bar. We arrived in good time, and in fine style with the roof down, but the misunderstanding—and his concern for my well-being—made me realize how caring and lovely he was. From that evening on we were on the phone or meeting up just about every day.

Ian's most common material for his comedy sketches was his family. He'd had a terrible childhood, he'd say, leaning on the mic with a small, wry smile, and then relate some awful, but awfully funny, incident. There was the time he fell out of the backseat of the car and his dad carried on driving because no one had noticed. The time he was going on a school trip and the minibus drove past his mum lying drunk on the pavement. How he and his sister loved *Coronation Street* because they knew when they heard the theme it would be safe to go home—Mum and Dad would have stopped fighting and gone off to work. For a long time I thought he was exaggerating—surely nobody's parents could be that bad. I didn't realize he was deliberately underplaying what he'd experienced.

Right the way through the course, I was still insisting to my friends that Ian and I were strictly platonic, but deep down I knew very quickly that we were soul mates. Whenever we went to see comedy, he'd do something nice for me—give me his coat when I was cold, buy me some flowers, or insist that he take me for a bite to eat before dropping me off at my flat. He was also an amazing cook. One day, when I was out on a course, he based himself for the afternoon at my flat, planning to take in a football game at my local pub later, as we were going to see some comedy together that evening. He'd been telling me all week about the crunch fixture that weekend—he was a huge Manchester United fan—but when I got home there was a pork and cider casserole steaming on the dinner table. He'd gone to the shops instead of the pub, bought a slow cooker and the ingredients and then stayed in all afternoon cooking.

Going from being friends to falling in love was only the smallest of steps.

Soon after the course finished, he asked me to go to the Dublin Writers Festival with him, and after that the Z4 frequently found itself parked outside my flat. Then, after a while, Ian would often leave me the car even when he was at home in the East Midlands, as he was worried about my old banger falling apart driving up the motorway to see him. Even my mum loved the BMW. I'd take her out into the countryside for a pub lunch, talking about Ian all the time. She didn't usually want me to put the top down because it played havoc with her hair. I'd got used to having haystack hair—it was worth it in my opinion.

Mum cried when I told her Ian and I were getting married.

"We probably won't be having kids," I said. We'd talked about it and thought it best not to, as we were both nearly forty (OK, let's not pretend, I was distinctly north of forty). "And he wants to have a wedding where it's just the two of us. We're thinking maybe of Hawaii."

I didn't tell her about Ian's particular reasons for wanting a small wedding, but Mum didn't mind. The important thing was that I'd found someone special. We weren't exactly young lovebirds, but I think that for her that made it even more precious.

Despite what I'd told my mum about not getting pregnant, and quashing her grandmotherly hopes in the process, by the time we got engaged I'd started to think—or maybe obsess would be a better word—about what a great dad Ian would make. He is so loving and kind and patient that any child would be lucky to have him for a father. We decided we'd let nature take its course. If I got pregnant, good. And if I didn't, we said that'd be fine too, though in my heart of hearts I yearned for a baby.

We flew to Waikiki in March, where the hotel beauty salon put my hair up, threading tropical flowers through the locks, and carefully covered my sunburn, where I'd got carried away snorkeling with turtles the day before, with cooling makeup. Ian helped me into my wedding dress— we'd both put on a bit of weight so our wedding clothes were a bit of a squeeze—I grabbed my colorful bouquet and we were off. Our photographer met us in the lobby and took us outside for extra photos while we waited for the vicar. Then we walked down to the beach and were officially wed. It was sunny, but with a few spits of rain. In one of the photos, I'm resting my head against Ian's chest and we are both looking as happy as can be; behind us, a rainbow arches across the sky.

Having a baby now would be the icing on the cake. When we got back to England, I spoke to my doctor and we went for a check-up. There wasn't anything wrong with either of us, he said.

"It'll just take a little time."

I started to take my temperature and chart my cycle. Poor Ian was expected to perform as and when required, wear loose boxers, not cycle too much and eat all the right foods.

Months passed, and I didn't get pregnant. We arranged to see a consultant at the hospital.

Ian drove me to the appointment, my haystack hair blowing in the wind, still newlyweds unburdened by cares. We left devastated. Having children was not going to be as easy as we'd hoped or expected. The blood tests I'd been given on day three of my cycle to check my hormones had not shown the results the consultants had hoped for. The levels just weren't right and they were causing my ovulation to be inhibited. It was hard to concentrate on the doctor's words. I listened in a daze of shocked misery. Perhaps, at my age, I should have been more prepared for disappointment, but being told you may not be able to have a baby isn't like, say, having your book rejected; it's a shock of such cataclysmic proportions that nothing can prepare you for it.

Our best hope was a drug called Clomid, which would increase my ovulation and—we all hoped—my fertility. It would be a year's course of drugs, with monthly screenings and blood tests at the hospital.

"The tests can vary slightly month by month," the nurse said, trying to console me.

We didn't have to decide there and then, but we both felt so heartbroken by this setback that I said on the spot I'd submit to the regime.

We drove home determined we'd beat the lengthening odds.

I thought about eggs, cycles, scans and pills constantly, which left me listless and unable to concentrate on my work. Ian shuttled to and from London on the train, and I moped around the house until, one night, he came through the door, still radiating the unexpected cold of the early September evening, and said: "Work's asked me to do two weeks in Japan, with a few days' stop-off at the office in Hong Kong on the way. Wanna come?"

Do fleas want to bite, or fish swim? Just because I was now a married woman didn't mean I wanted to stop exploring.

It was in Japan that my conversion to dog lover began.

While Ian was working in the day, I battled jetlag by throwing myself into the frenetic stream of existence that is Tokyo. Traveling on the metro every day, I visited the teeming shopping area of Shibuya, the sprawling temple at Asakusa and the Tokyo Tower. I marveled at the costumes of the Harajuku teenagers, took photographs of some shy trainee sumo wrestlers outside the Sumo Wrestling Arena and had my first taste of a kabuki show—as translated by a sweet eighty-year-old Japanese lady sitting next to me.

Toward the end of the week, exhausted, I visited the island of Odaiba, just off Tokyo, for some relaxation, and experienced a traditional Japanese spa. Men and women were strictly segregated, given kimonos and flip-flops before a careful washing ritual, supervised by a matronly figure, and nude bathing in the single-sex area. It was heaven. I even forgave them for saying I needed an extra-large kimono.

"You have to give it a try," I told Ian, and so the following Saturday we set off.

Strolling from the ferry terminal, we'd only gone a short way, and were nowhere near the spa, when we saw a long, snaking queue of people patiently waiting outside a shop. Above the entrance was a picture of a dog wearing a hat, and in the window lots of pictures of small, adorably cute pooches. Gradually, we realized we'd stumbled across a rent-a-dog shop—somewhere you could hire a dog to walk, pet and play with. An hour of fun, relaxation and stress relief with a lovable mutt, with none of the long-term hassles of owning one.

"Do we want to wait?"

We looked at each other, grinned and took our place in the queue of Japanese adults and children, all waiting with barely suppressed excitement to spend some time with a puppy. There was plenty of time to look at the pictures of the available dogs as we slowly edged around the corner and into the shop, but for me there was no contest: a long-eared, short-legged, caramel-coated, big-eyed pooch stared beseechingly at me from his photo through the glass. Written above his photo was his name, but although we'd learned to speak quite a lot of Japanese before we'd arrived we weren't able to read it. Finally, when it was our turn, we pointed to his picture and were told by the beaming kennel maid that his name was Goro. But unfortunately we couldn't have Goro yet: all the dogs were out, and our names were added to the list for the second shift of dog walking.

"Come back in an hour; he will be waiting," she said. Then, seeing our indecision: "Go and eat something," and we obediently trotted over to a nearby café. I ate udon, and Ian ordered noodles too, but just stirred them around awkwardly in his bowl with his chopsticks. The hour dragged by.

When we returned, the beaming kennel maid gave us all the kit, essentials that a dog like Goro might need: a poo bag, along with strict instructions that it must be used, and a little shovel for picking up the deposit; a bottle of water and a bowl; and a small, garish bag of treats emblazoned with katakana characters. If Goro got tired, we were told in Japanese and broken English, we were to carry him.

"You must not scold him."

Scold? Ian and I looked at each other. The possibility hadn't even entered our heads.

"And you bring him back." She pointed at her watch.

We promised we wouldn't be late, and after paying a hefty deposit (though there was no danger of any dognapping: there were no cars on the island and the ferry was the only way off it) Goro finally made his entrance. We were just as awestruck and excited as all the Japanese people we'd watched leaving with their hired dogs before us.

"He's so small."

"And so cute."

"His eyes . . ."

"His coat's so soft . . ."

Goro nonchalantly looked gorgeous. We were just two more of the many people who came to the island and fell in love with him and his friends at the dog-hire shop every week.

Outside the shop, we looked at each other: what on earth were we meant to do now? All we'd seen of the island was the beach where we'd got off the ferry, the dog-hire place, the restaurant and the shops adjoining it—plus what we thought might possibly be a rent-a-cat place. Although we hadn't seen anyone walking about with a cat, anything seemed possible. We headed to the beach, nodding and smiling to other dog hirers we passed, proud, like them, of our new "dog owner" status. At this point Goro, who had seen it all before and knew far more than us about what was supposed to happen during an hour's hire, decided he'd had enough of walking. We tried tempting him to budge with some of his treats, but he was having none of it. In his eyes it was very clear: there was no bad feeling—he simply didn't feel like walking anymore and therefore he wasn't going to.

"Come on, Goro."

Goro stayed where he was.

"You try."

I held on to the lead.

"Come on, Goro. Come on, there's a good boy."

Goro looked at me with his beautiful melting-chocolate brown eyes. I crouched down and he waddled over to me.

"Are you tired out?" I said, stroking him.

That he really seemed to enjoy. His head came up for more and I swear he had a smile on his face.

"Would you like to be carried?" I said, and lifted him into my arms. Goro was the perfect dog for carrying.

He snuggled into me and didn't wriggle at all—apart from when he tried to give my ear a lick.

"What shall we do now?" I said.

"Pub?" The Englishman's unfailing antenna for the hostelry had located one a little farther down the beach. As we sat down outside, people at the other tables made appreciative noises and smiled at Goro, who accepted his due and sat on the tabletop, soaking up the attention while eating the tiny pieces of chicken we offered him.

All too soon our hour was up and we watched him walk back through the partition to his kennel with regret. If we had a dog, I said, maybe he'd be like Goro. Ian, though, couldn't see himself owning such a little dog: he wanted something bigger and "more manly." And, anyway, having a dog would be such a tie—we'd never have been able to come to Japan if we'd had a dog at home. Now wasn't the time, but maybe one day. Maybe one day we'd have a dog like Goro.

By the middle of the next week, Ian's business in Japan was done and it was time for him to fly home. I, however, had bought a round-the-world ticket and was taking an extended holiday. My flight left almost a day later than his, so I kissed Ian goodbye, put him in a taxi to Narita and went back to the hotel room where I immediately changed the screensaver on my laptop to a photo of him and Goro. I would look at it frequently in the weeks to come; every time I did, it made me smile.

I flew to countries where I already had friends—America, Ecuador and New Zealand. In Ecuador I stayed with an old school-friend, Susan, a midwife who'd been trying to have children for most of her adult life. She'd tried just about everything, from diet to acupuncture to reflexology, as well as an endless round of fertility drugs and IVF treatments. Her husband, Graham, worked overseas and she'd been a midwife in Brazil, France, Peru and now Ecuador. Susan took me with her to the small, privately funded orphanage where she'd started volunteering. I just loved helping out at the orphanage for the week I was there: I've always had an affinity with children and for years taught children with profound learning difficulties.

Susan was hoping that now she and her husband were in Ecuador they'd be able to adopt there. They'd inquired about adopting in England the year before but had been told that they wouldn't even be eligible to start the process until they'd had a year free of fertility treatments—and Susan hadn't a clue where they'd be by then. It had been a very disheartening experience.

At the orphanage there was a six-month-old baby girl who had been given up for adoption. "I'm hoping they'll let me adopt the baby," Susan said. "She's perfect."

One little girl was so pleased to see Susan she crawled across the floor as fast as she could to get to her. Eliana was almost three and had had a difficult start in life. Both of her parents were long-term drug addicts who'd been arrested for possession when Eliana was a baby and sent to prison. Eliana had, while in prison with her mother, caught pneumonia three times and had been transferred to the hospital where she became malnourished due to lack of care by her relatives, surviving for days at a time with no food and only an IV drip. When the orphanage was called in, nobody had changed her nappy for a week, and she looked more like a newborn than a seven-month-old, so small and fragile was she.

The prognosis for Eliana had not been good. She had never been expected to hold her head up, walk or speak, and she was never expected to progress further than a typical four-month-old baby due to the damage caused by her parents' drug use.

But no one had told that to Eliana, and she was setting about proving them wrong. When I met her, she'd learned to crawl, despite damage to her hip joints, and understood what was being said. She let everyone know how she felt without the need for words and ate her solid food with gusto.

She wriggled across the floor toward us, absolutely determined to get to her favorite person, and was grinning with delight when she reached Susan.

Eliana was clinging to Susan's legs and looking up at her with her big brown eyes, pleading. Susan knew what she wanted.

"OK, we'll do some coloring."

Susan was full of positivity. She'd been through so many difficulties and heartaches, and was completely devoted to all the children in her care; and now, after so long, it seemed as if she and her husband would finally be getting their dream. I left on the plane home newly convinced that, despite everything, things would work out for Ian and me too.

A few weeks after I arrived home, Ian gave a shout from upstairs and came running down with the paper.

"Helper Dogs are opening a new satellite center in the East Midlands. Look, they've put an advert in."

We'd seen a program on TV about Helper Dogs—one of the many charities that provides expertly trained dogs for disabled people—and had been amazed at what the dogs were able to learn and the bond that developed between the dogs and their owners.

"It couldn't hurt to go and see," I said, taking the paper from Ian and looking at the square-bordered advert.

"Couldn't hurt at all," Ian agreed.

The advert said Helper Dogs wanted volunteers in our area to become puppy parents. Puppy parents looked after puppies for six months or so, before the puppy either went on to stay with another volunteer family, or to undertake its advanced training at the Helper Dogs HQ in Hertfordshire.

The new center was holding an open afternoon in a few days' time for prospective parents. However, since I'd never been responsible for a dog for more than an hour, we decided to phone to find out more. Nervous, I dialed the number and waited.

"Answering machine," I said, putting the phone down. I didn't want to leave a message.

A few minutes later, it rang. A Scottish voice, amid a

commotion and sounds of rustling and barking in the background:

"Hi, I'm Jamie, I run the Fenston Helper Dogs Center. Sorry, couldn't get to the phone quick enough. Are you interested in being a puppy parent?"

"Yes. Yes, I am. Well, maybe . . . I'm thinking of coming to the open afternoon—where exactly do I go?"

Ian couldn't come because he had to work, so I drove over to the center before its grand opening to check out exactly where it was. Still, I ended up being late on the day and just caught the official opening by the mayor. Then Helper Dogs gave a demonstration. I watched in amazement as dogs opened doors and turned on lights and helped their owners to take off their socks, shoes, hats, and coats. They could find keys, bring the phone, press emergency alarm buttons, take washing from washing machines, and make their disabled owner's life better in a hundred different ways.

Everyone who had a Helper Dog sang its praises.

"I couldn't go out before I had him, but now I go out every day," one lady said. "He's my life."

"If it wasn't for her, I'd have no reason to wake up in the morning," said a man confined to a wheelchair by cerebral palsy.

A young man with no arms and legs had tears streaming down his face as he told us how his dog brought his prosthetic limbs to him each morning.

"She's everything to me. My whole world."

I blinked back my own tears and swallowed hard. I now wanted to volunteer to become a puppy parent more than ever.

2

Rusty, the curly coated golden retriever, looked up at me with his big brown eyes, silently beseeching me for one of the treats I had secreted in my pocket. We were in the Helper Dogs center and I was putatively in charge of Rusty at an obedience class, but I couldn't shake the feeling that really he was in charge of me.

It had been a whirlwind few weeks. After my first visit to the center, I had come home ready to beg Ian to agree to taking in a puppy. Luckily, he'd guessed as much and had put a bottle of champagne in the fridge as I'd left the house. We'd decided to take the leap, opened the champagne and toasted becoming puppy parents. Since then, I'd been driving to see Helper Dogs once or twice a week, and, at Jamie's suggestion, I'd started attending puppy-training classes and was throwing myself into a new doggy world. I still didn't have a puppy, hence there was Rusty. Rusty's family had divorced when he was a puppy and neither husband nor wife had been able to keep him. He had ended up with Jamie and was an ideal training partner for me because he could do everything perfectly already.

November was dragging to its end. It was dark and cold, and the Christmas shopping hadn't kicked in yet—let alone the Christmas cheer—so I was pleased to have something nice to do. Having had a cursory look around the local pet shop, it was already promising to be an expensive Christmas:

we had puppy supplies to buy and a long list of home improvements on which to get started. When I phoned Jamie to put our names on the official puppy parent waiting list, he had announced that he was going to pay us a home visit to oversee the preparations that would ready the house for its new occupant, and to chat about what being a puppy parent would involve. Two days of extreme tidying ensued, during which I did my best to imagine what the perfect puppy home would look like, and then tried to re-create it in our little terraced house.

"He's not going to be looking in our cupboards," Ian had said, trying to reason with me as I chucked away out-of-date spices and piles of old magazines. Still, it was important to put our best face on, I thought, as I invested in a new mop, cleaning products and dusters. Escape-proofing the garden was most important, I decided, and there was an interesting-looking space behind the shed and garage wall where an inquisitive puppy could easily squeeze in and get stuck. Fortunately, the pimply assistant in the DIY super-store had been only too happy to supply piles of fencing and a padlock for the back gate.

Jamie's visit came around quickly. On the appointed Friday, the doorbell rang, and I opened the door to see him standing there in his Helper Dogs fleece, jeans and sensible boots, confident I'd done everything short of moving house to be as ready as possible for the pup. I affected the nonchalant air of a person who had always lived in serene tidiness.

"Hello, sorry I'm late. Bit of a dog emergency," Jamie said as he breezed in.

I rearranged the biscuits I'd bought in case he was peckish, to cover for the fact that I'd been waiting anxiously since breakfast. It was nearly lunchtime. Perhaps I should offer him a sandwich? Come to think of it, I wasn't sure I had any bread. How could I have forgotten the bread? I hoped he wouldn't think the worst of me because of it. Back turned, heart racing, I boiled the kettle, while he told me a little about what being a puppy parent would entail.

"You'll either be given a very young puppy, which you'll keep for around six months."

I nodded. "Cu-u-ute."

"Or else you'll be given an older one that you'll keep till it's about a year old and goes off for its final training."

Jamie took a swig of tea.

"I'd like a younger one," I said.

"Depends what's available," Jamie said. "Head Office decides who gets what, not me. Young ones are sweet but a lot of work—and very time consuming. Little puppies need to be taken out to the loo every few hours, so there won't be much sleep for you for the first few weeks . . ."

I didn't care about that.

". . . and there will probably be more than a few little accidents in the house . . ."

"We're thinking of getting laminate flooring."

". . . and little puppies chew. A lot." He'd spotted the computer wires. Ian was obsessed with gadgets and hung on to his old computers like they were his children. There were wires and leads for every occasion in every corner. They seemed to have a life of their own, reproducing and popping up in unexpected places as soon as your back was turned.

"I'll get Ian to box them in."

"You'll need a gate to stop the puppy from going up the

stairs," Jamie continued. "And if you're given a baby puppy it'll need to sleep in your room for the first few nights, so you'll hear it when it wakes up . . ."

I nodded.

"And you'll need to take it to the toilet straightaway so it doesn't ever mess in its bed—you'll need to carry it up and down the stairs. Stairs aren't good for a little puppy's joints, especially the Labradors, Golden Retrievers and Labradoodles we use."

We took our tea out for a tour of the garden, a square lawn fringed with dying bedding plants, a new rockery with perky shoots poking through, an arbor seat nestled into the bushes, a patio, a shed and a couple of trees.

"Where's the toilet area going?" Jamie asked. Helper Dogs needed an area covered with play sand or bark chippings, at least a meter square. I'd never toilet trained a dog before, but it couldn't be that hard, I told myself.

"Under the lilac tree?" I said. The tree was near the house and the patio.

Jamie frowned. "No, I don't think that'll work. You don't want to be sitting almost on top of the puppy's loo, do you? The ideal place, I suppose, would be down there." He pointed to our recently built rockery. "But it'd mean . . ."

"Oh, we're not bothered about that old thing," I said.

We went back inside and I made some more tea.

"I'll need to meet Ian, of course," he said. "Bring him along to the center some time."

My head was spinning. There was so much to think about and organize. So many things to buy for such a small creature.

He caught my pensive expression. "Don't worry, I'm sure you'll be great," he said. "I'm just a bit concerned because you haven't had a dog before."

I bit my tongue and resisted saying anything about Goro. "When d'you think we'll get our puppy?"

"Not for a while yet—maybe sometime after Christmas. It depends when they're available. Could be March."

That long? I sighed.

So here I was, three weeks later, filling my waiting time by learning about dogs at the Helper Dog class. Rusty now made me feel very welcome at the center. He recognized me as the lady who brought him nice things, and he hurried over every time I walked through the door. He'd do anything for a treat and spent his life on a diet. I wasn't so keen on, indeed was a little frightened of, Jamie's other dog, a German Shepherd called Queenie. Barely used to dogs at all, I certainly wasn't habituated to gruff Alsatians. How did easygoing Rusty manage to live with her? I never saw the two of them playing together, and although she was often at the Helper Dogs center, the other dogs treated her with deference or gave her a wide berth.

Each Helper Dogs session began with tea and coffee and the chance for puppy parents to report on how their puppies were progressing. We were early, so next to me and Rusty there were only two young puppies, Dylan and Daisy, and an older puppy called Arnie, who'd been pulled out of advanced training for a while because he kept barking all the time. Julia had Dylan, a Flat-coated Retriever. He had long legs that reminded me of Bambi. Len, a retired insurance salesman, had Daisy, a cute, chocolate-brown Labrador. I loved hearing how the puppies got on each week.

"I thought you might be interested in this," Julia said to me one week, and she gave me a timesheet of everything she did with Dylan during a typical day. It looked like a full-time job with a strong emphasis on toilet training.

I wasn't quite so keen on the other class I went to each week—the clicker training class. Or so keen on Frank, the other Helper Dogs official who had moved down from Scotland with Jamie and now shared management of the training center. While Jamie concentrated on the Helper Dogs work, Frank ran the regular obedience classes for dogs of all kinds in the daytimes. These included agility and clicker work. Clicker work involved clicking a small hand-held device followed immediately by giving the dog a treat. The clicking sound meant "good work."

"The idea is that you reward Rusty as soon as he does what you asked of him," Frank sighed as he explained it for the twentieth time, loudly, in front of the whole class. "If you're late with your click or click for inappropriate behavior then your dog will never learn what's expected from him—will he?"

I looked down at Rusty. He gave me a consoling look back. If it wasn't for Rusty, I might have been thrown out of the class as a hopeless case. Rusty was so smart he got just about everything right, even when I clicked in the wrong place.

As the class was finishing, I saw Ian at the door. We were off to the coach station to pick his mother up. Her visit was a big deal; because they'd treated him unspeakably when he was little, Ian still had trouble spending much time with his parents. His father, Bernie, and aunt, Mabel, had been to visit while I was in Japan, so I'd been spared some awkward family time—although Auntie Mabel had often looked after him and his sister during the toughest of times. Now, Barbara was coming to stay, despite Ian putting her off as much as he could. We were both apprehensive, though I was determined to make the best of the few days and get them over with without a fuss. We'd decided to go to the station together for moral support.

While he waited, Ian made a big fuss of Queenie, who lapped up his attention, rolling onto her back to have her stomach rubbed.

"Funny that," Jamie said. "She doesn't usually like strangers—especially not men—apart from me and Frankie, of course." He smiled and nodded his head. Ian had passed the approval test.

Barbara's coach from Stockport had arrived early, so she was waiting, smoking a cigarette, when we pulled up at the station. She was a wrinkled sickly looking woman, so tiny that you wouldn't expect her presence to be so disruptive. Ian still had trouble telling me about—or even remembering— the worst bits of his upbringing, and it was only under special circumstances that he would see her at all. As the coach driver pulled a large suitcase from the hold, she lit another cigarette. Ian hated smoking—perhaps because when he was little she'd spent all her kids' dinner money on cigarettes and sent them to school hungry—and had said to her before she came that if she smoked in the house he'd send her packing. I took the suitcase and put it in the boot. It was as light as anything; she couldn't have much in it.

Ian's mum and dad hadn't been good parents and now expected him to sort out all their problems—financial or otherwise—for them, but all I had been able to see, when he'd finally taken me to Stockport to meet them for the first time just before we got engaged, were two sick old people who tried as hard as they could to be nice to me. At first, I'd wondered why Ian hadn't cut all ties with his family or stayed to start a new life in America where he'd lived for a few years, and I felt if he could still be civil to them then I certainly could. A long while later he told me that he had thought about not telling me about his parents when we'd first met, and pretending they were dead. I'm glad he didn't. I was the only girlfriend that he'd ever taken to meet his family.

At home, Barbara admired the house, what she called the "woman's touch" I'd brought to her son's bachelor pad, but mainly she sat in the garden, drinking cups of tea and smoking. I took pity on her and sat with her awhile. She said she was trying to give up, and she seemed sincere. With her long auburn hair, she reminded me a bit of my sweet grandmother, and I tried my best to be pleasant to her, despite Ian's obvious antipathy and mistrust. We'd told my mum that we were trying for a child, and all the complications that were now arriving with it, but had said nothing to his family. I broke the news to her and found her surprisingly sympathetic.

"You're like me, maternal—you'll make a lovely mother," she said.

I sincerely hoped this was true in the way she'd intended it to be, and not true to Ian's experiences.

Barbara patted my hand. "It'll be your turn soon."

I was pleasantly surprised that things were going so smoothly. However, at some point while talking, she swapped her cup of tea for a glass of wine, then an empty glass for a full one, and the bottle was soon finished. As she wobbled off to bed, she said to me that she'd accompany me to the hospital in the morning, where I was having my monthly hormone check. As I agreed and said goodnight, I saw Ian, across the room, raise his eyebrows and, when she'd gone upstairs, sigh with relief.

In the morning, Barbara didn't appear the worse for wear, and it was nice having her along with me at the hospital. I didn't like going much; there was a lot of waiting around, and the blood tests were often painful. Sometimes, too, I had to go to the Obstetrics and Gynecology department, which was always difficult. I was glad I wasn't going there with Barbara. It was hard seeing the pregnant women and thinking that'll be me one day—hopefully soon. Sometimes women would come out of the treatment rooms crying.

The monthly tests were precautions to check how the Clomid was working, and that it wasn't overstimulating my body. I took Clomid on days three to seven of my cycle to increase the process of egg maturation in the ovaries, then, on day twenty-one, the hospital took blood to measure my progesterone levels and performed scans to make sure no complications were occurring.

Aside from the big risks, there were also side effects. I had mood swings, nausea and occasional vomiting and, less often, breast tenderness, headaches and general fatigue. I also gained some weight, but thankfully my body responded well to a low—50 mg—dose of the drug. This month, as with the previous month, the doctor was pleased with my progress. Taking well to the drug was only the first step, but it was an important one.

That evening we ran out of wine and Barbara decided to try the mint-chocolate Baileys I'd been given for my birthday back in March and hadn't got around to opening. I was sitting chatting to Ian, and she took the bottle outside with her while she was smoking. A while later Barbara came back inside and I was horrified when she spoke to see that she was frothing at the mouth. I asked her if she was OK. She slurred that she was, but that she thought she might be allergic to the minted Baileys. At the thought, she looked at the bottle, held it up and shook it. There was none left.

"Mum, you're drunk," said Ian, slipping unhappily into an old and familiar role.

He prised the bottle from her hand, took her to the bathroom to clean up and then helped her upstairs to bed. He came down some while later looking drained, and we hugged. A while later I went upstairs to check she was OK. Barbara heard me outside the door and shouted: "Come in, love!"

I opened the door and peeped around. She was in bed with the lamp on and looked a little better.

"I've had a vision," she said. "You're going to have a little girl."

Despite everything she'd done to Ian when he was little, everything she'd put us through that evening, and everything she'd drunk in the past two days, I wanted to believe her. I really, really wanted to believe in her vision. A little girl would be perfect.

"And I saw a robin in your garden," Barbara said softly. "Robins always bring good luck."

I shut the door, tiptoed back down the stairs and cried on Ian's shoulder.

I couldn't sleep that night because I had stomach cramps, and the next morning I was devastated when I started to bleed. No chance of getting pregnant this month. I tried to put on a brave face in front of Barbara and didn't tell her what had happened. Barbara remembered nothing about the allergic reaction, or her vision. She'd had a lovely night's sleep, which is more than we'd managed. That afternoon, Ian and I took her back to the coach station, waved goodbye and started to get on with our life again.

3

It was a few weeks before Christmas, and I was trying my best to squeeze my broken-down old car into the crowded Helper Dogs car park. Getting out wasn't a problem, though: I was usually the last to leave. I smiled at Frank as I walked into the training room. He smiled back. I tried to believe that he didn't mind having such a clicker-klutz in his class, but I wasn't convinced, fully aware as I now was that training the puppy was less than half the battle. Rusty was very pleased to see me too. I was an easy target—a free lunch.

Across the room, Darcy, a usually mild-tempered, chocolate Labrador cross, barked aggressively at Zack, a young German Shepherd, and tried to lunge at him. Zack, probably terrified at going to a new class, barked and snarled back at Darcy.

"Turn your dogs' faces away!" Frank shouted at both owners.

Darcy's owner managed it but Zack's didn't. Frank was there in a flash. He took Zack's lead from him.

"You don't pull them away with the lead, because the dog will just go in a circle and end up facing the other dog again, do you see?"

The owner, red in the face with embarrassment, nodded. He looked like he really, really wished he hadn't come to class today. I knew how he felt.

Rusty sniffed at my pocket for treats.

I found Zack and Darcy's aggressive behavior frightening. How would I deal with some aggressive wild dog when walking my new puppy in the park? I definitely wasn't going to grab its head and turn it around.

I gave Rusty some more treats. Three, to be exact, and we hadn't even started the class proper, more to comfort myself than him—he was an old hand, completely unfazed by the other dogs' behavior. But he was very hungry. Hadn't he eaten breakfast? Usually he was enthusiastic about treats, but today he was going wild. I was running out of treats fast. We had another packet, but they were over near Zack, whose owner was furiously practicing being calm. I didn't want to disturb them.

"Now we'll practice following the stick," Frank said.

Rusty was excellent at stick-following, but I'd given him his last treat. The bag was empty.

"Or actually, Meg, I'd like you to show everyone how good Rusty is at spinning," Frank said.

Rusty was good at that too. He would usually spin around with just a command from me and the tiniest twist of my finger.

"Twist, Rusty," I said, and twirled my index finger around to show him what I wanted him to do.

Rusty did it perfectly and then waited for his treat.

"One more time," Frank said. "Just use your voice this time."

"Twist, Rusty." *Please.*

Rusty was confused. Where was his treat? He was supposed to have a treat. He didn't twist and tried barking at me instead.

"Wait for Rusty to think it through and then ask him again," Frank said.

I waited. Rusty got even more desperate for his treats and jumped up at me to remind me.

"Twist, Rusty."

I waited. The rest of the class and Frank waited. I knew Rusty wasn't going to twist. He wasn't going to do anything without a treat.

Frank folded his arms and looked cross. I didn't want Rusty to be in trouble because of me. I bit the bullet.

"I'm out of treats," I told Frank. "Would it be OK if I went past Zack to get the other ones?" I felt like Oliver Twist asking for more gruel. My classmates all found it very funny.

Frank handed me the treats and then fortunately became distracted when Darcy started snarling at a small white Yorkshire Terrier.

"Turn your dog's face away from the other!" he barked.

Rusty put out his paw. I tried not to give him another treat. He gave me a hard stare.

A few days later we set off to see Ian's family in Stockport for a pre-Christmas visit. I was wearing the warm coat I usually wore when I went to dog training, as Stockport could be freezing. Plus we were driving up in our convertible, and I did so like having the roof down, mid-December or not.

We hadn't gone far and were on a busy dual carriageway when I saw a very young German Shepherd puppy racing down a thin strip of path and scrub in front of us, its lead trailing behind it. At any second it could run into the road and be crushed.

"Stop the car!" I shouted.

Ian swerved into a lay-by and I jumped out.

"Come on, here, puppy, what's this?" I said in my "what's this exciting thing I've got?" voice.

The puppy trotted over. I reached into my pocket and found one of Rusty's treats. It sniffed at it but then snuggled into me instead. I could feel its little heart beating very fast. The training hadn't been a complete waste of time. I was getting better with dogs, more natural and more able to gain their trust. I could feel my confidence grow.

Ian came over and knelt down beside us.

"Hello, puppy," he said. The puppy wagged its tail and licked his face.

"It's much too young to be out running down a busy road. Where are its owners?" I said. I was very angry; anything could have happened. "We'd make much better parents."

For a second Ian and I looked at each other, the same thought crossing our minds. This could be our puppy. Its owners were nowhere to be seen.

I sighed. We both knew we couldn't do it.

Ian went back to the car and I walked up the grassy bank. A man in the distance was walking our way, but unhurried. He didn't look like he was in the panic he should have been in.

"Is this your dog?" I shouted. He didn't reply but carried on walking toward us.

"The wife would've killed me if I'd come back without it," he said when he eventually reached me.

I handed over the puppy's lead and watched as the puppy bounced away with the man, before going back to the car. Ian gave me a long look before he eased the car back into the traffic flowing north.

"Soon we'll have our own," he said.

Meeting the puppy was the highlight of our weekend away. Soon couldn't be soon enough.

Even so, a shock ran through me when Jamie rang a few days after we got back.

"Meg! Thank goodness you're in," Jamie's familiar Scottish burr shouted down the phone. "There's been a mix-up—the puppies have arrived early. I need you to come and pick yours up from the training center . . . now?"

I looked at the piles of laminate flooring, still in plastic wrappers, waiting to be laid in the kitchen. Then there were the computer wires that hadn't yet been boxed in. The gaps in the fence at the back of the garden. The million and one things I'd put on the list but hadn't got around to. There was also the ski stuff at the bottom of the bed, in the shed and piling up in the hall ready for a Christmas ski break. We wouldn't be going to the Alps, then. The house wasn't ready yet—we weren't ready yet—but we couldn't turn it away. My heart was thumping like a fifteen-year-old going on a first date. Would the puppy like me? Please let it like me. I was going to be a first-time puppy parent. A puppy mum.

A quarter of an hour later, at the center, I had Emma in my arms. She wriggled sleepily and gave a sniffle that melted my heart. Below, in the crate, her brother was shifting sleepily on the small piece of blanket that had been cut from the one they'd shared with their mum and the litter only a short time before.

The puppies had been donated to Helper Dogs by Guide Dogs for the Blind. All the assistance-dogs charities, in fact, tried to help each other out and share spare dogs if a litter came unexpectedly. Each one had its preferred breeders, known for providing healthy dogs with good temperaments, and would have a standing order to take whole litters at a time. Then if, for some reason, they didn't need the dogs, they were loath to see them go to waste and would contact another charity's trainer. Good puppies cost £500 or more to buy but would cost ten times that to train, so it was crucial to start off with the best recruits possible.

I could hardly believe I'd soon be taking Emma home. That she'd be mine and Ian's to love and take care of, our own little puppy-girl.

A cloud passed in front of the sun and Jamie shivered.

"That'll probably be the last of the sun for today. Let's get the puppies inside. There's a few bits and pieces I need to give you before you take Emma home."

In the staff room, with Emma back in the crate, Jamie started clipping sheets of paper into a folder.

"You'll need a Helper Dogs manual," he said, holding a thick booklet up. "Make sure you study it. It has all you need to know in it. And report forms—these need to be done every week for the first few weeks and every month from then on."

"Right."

"They learn so much so fast—you'll be amazed."

He handed me a bag of dog food.

"This should last you until the next Helper Dogs meeting. Mix a little of this in with the brand her breeder's been giving her when you give her her next meal, and then a little more of our food and a little less of the breeder's food at each meal after that until she's only having our food."

Helper Dogs provided all the basic food, but not treats, and they'd pay any vet's bills. They also provided a crate for the puppy, and bedding.

"And you'll need a water bowl and a food bowl," Jamie said, and went to find some. The Helper Dogs training center, being a regular dog-training center as well, had a range of dog items for sale.

I looked at Emma's brother, sleeping so peacefully next to her.

"What's going to happen to Emma's brother?"

"Coming home with me and Frank tonight and then his puppy parent, Liz, will pick him up tomorrow."

"Seems a shame to split them up . . . I could—"

Jamie looked horrified. "No, no, no—believe me, one puppy is enough for now!"

Emma and her brother carried on sleeping. "And you'll need to buy her a collar and lead—Helper Dogs will reimburse you. Make sure you buy a very soft one—the softest you can find."

He looked around, as if searching for something more to say or do, some more advice to impart to a novice puppy parent. Delaying the moment that I was both nervously waiting for and hoping would never come.

"Right," he decided abruptly. "That's about it, then."

"I can take her home?"

"You can take her home."

I put the assembled crate in the back of my car along with Emma's comfort blanket and a toy, and then I carried Emma over to the car.

"That's it, there's a good girl."

She was very calm, although her heart was beating very

fast, and she didn't wriggle as I put her into the crate.

I turned into the main road and she started to cry. Immediately, I wanted to cry too. I couldn't bear it. I'd have to stop but not yet: the road was too busy. I'd need to turn off, but where? The crying stopped. Emma had fallen asleep.

Twenty minutes later, I pulled up outside our house and carried Emma up the garden path.

"This is going to be your new home," I told her, carrying her into the house, fragile and tiny in my arms. As soon as we got in, I took Emma out to the toilet area and she used it. For the next few weeks I was to take Emma to the toilet area after every meal, when she woke up from a sleep and when she'd been getting overexcited.

I phoned Ian. "Babes, I've got the puppy. She's a little girl and her name's Emma, but we need some more things for her from the pet shop."

I gave him a list of items to pick up on his way home, then carefully measured out exactly the amount of food she was supposed to have and poured it into her bowl. She sniffed at it but didn't eat any, although she did have a few sips of water before curling up and going to sleep.

Emma was awake and full of life by the time Ian came home.

"Hello, little puppy girl," he said, kneeling down in his best work suit so he could pet her. "Welcome to your new home."

She snuggled into him and I felt a lump in my throat. She was so perfect and so tiny.

"What have I got for you?" Ian said, and pulled a name tag, a soft blanket and a cushion bed from the pet-shop bags. "They said they could tell I was a new dad!" he said, sounding slightly miffed as he opened the third bag of presents and treats for Emma. "Look—they even had puppy milk."

Emma immediately pounced on a brown dog toy that was almost the same size as her and started to play fight with it while making little puppy squeaks. The dog squeaked back and she sat down fast, shocked. A few hours later Ian brought the crate in from the car and carried it up the stairs. It was time for bed. Jamie had warned us we probably wouldn't get much sleep during the first few weeks, but I didn't care. We had our puppy—who cared about sleep?

"Night night, Emma," we said, and put her in her crate at the foot of our bed. She was curled up on the small piece of blanket with the scent of her mum on it.

That night we slept with our heads at the foot of the bed so we could be as near as possible to her.

"She'll probably cry during the first night," Jamie had said. "But don't worry. It's a big thing for a tiny puppy. It'll be the first night she hasn't spent with her mum and her brothers and sisters."

But Emma didn't cry. She curled up and went to sleep. I tried to sleep too, but I couldn't. I didn't want to miss hearing her if she needed me, so I listened to her tiny breathing as she slept.

An hour or so later she woke up and gave a whimper.

"It's all right, Emma," I said. "It's OK."

I lifted her little warm body out of the crate and hurried downstairs, padding past the Christmas tree and its winking multicolored lights in the corner. We'd only just got out the back door when she did her business.

I looked up at the sky, standing in my dressing gown and overcoat underneath the frosty stars. Emma followed me on a little trip of discovery around our garden before I sat down on our arbor seat, tucked into the bushes, and lifted her onto my lap. No need to rush back to bed just yet. She snuggled into me and I undid my coat, placed her inside and did the zip up, so she peeked out like a baby kangaroo. Pretty soon she fell asleep. I looked down and knew our decision to become puppy parents had been a very good one. I was already totally in love with her.

I felt a cold spot on my face and then another. It was snowing. Just lightly. Probably not enough to settle.

"We're very pleased you've come to live with us," I whispered.

4

Christmas Day with a puppy was like none I'd experienced before. For starters, it began much, much earlier. Barely was it daylight than the alarm had already gone and I'd trooped out into the garden so that Emma could do her business on her frosty toilet area. I'd gone back to bed in the hope of catching a few more Christmas winks and a snuggle with Ian, but she was yapping, jumping and eager for fun at the bottom of the stairs. She was full of the joys of only being eight weeks in this world, and, although she didn't know Christmas from any other day, even a normal day dramatically extended her experience of the world and held plenty of surprises and adventures. She trotted behind me as I got her breakfast ready: two-thirds of a bowl of Helper Dogs' food, one-third of the food she'd been eating at her breeder's. She loved her food, but even as a little puppy girl she was very ladylike, eating it delicately rather than wolfing it down as fast as she could as some puppies do.

Later, we'd wiped the sleep from our eyes and restored our equanimity with a small glass of bubbly, and thus our small family gathered around the tree together for the first time.

"Open this one," Ian said, handing me a present.

Inside was a small cuddly smiling Labrador toy.

"I didn't think we'd have Emma yet," Ian said sheepishly.

The toy Lab caught Emma's eye right away, and she began jumping and begging to play with it. Surely Ian must have bought it for her? As far as she was concerned, all nice things to play with in the world were hers.

"Can I?" I said.

"If you want to. It came from the pet shop."

Emma already had quite a collection—her small toy box was overflowing—but we couldn't resist giving her more.

"Here you are," I said, after checking it didn't have any parts that might be bitten off and swallowed by a rambunctious pup. Fortunately, its eyes were made of material rather than plastic buttons. It was cute but didn't look that robust. In Emma's current exuberant form, I gave it about three days. I had already been busy performing emergency surgery on a couple of toys who'd come into the sewing ER, covered in dribble and spilling their insides out after a particularly enthusiastic mauling.

Soon enough, though, Emma abandoned the Lab—whom we christened Spiky, after a peculiar tuft of hair on his brow—and turned her attention to the wrapping paper. She mainly liked the tearing sound, and attacking it as it drifted to the floor and collected in flurries around the sofa.

Sometimes I was shocked at how much I loved her already and how protective I was. It was an anxious love too—especially on Boxing Day when I thought I'd lost her. I left the room to answer the phone and then ran upstairs to check something on the computer. When I came back down, she was nowhere to be seen, and the toy Lab was looking lonesome and forlorn on the floor.

"Emma?" I said. She wasn't in the living room. I hurried

into the kitchen. She wasn't there either, but the back door was open a crack. I went outside, scanned the garden quickly, but she wasn't there either, and I started to panic, really panic. I felt sick, and a lump rose in my throat that made it hard to breathe. She was so lovely; it wasn't hard to believe that someone would have wanted to take her and who else would be wandering around on Boxing Day except somebody bad? She was so tiny, so vulnerable, so trusting—what if she was lost? Cold and afraid.

There was a small gap in the hedge. Small enough for a tiny puppy to squeeze through if she was determined, and Emma could be very determined when she chose to be.

I ran next door and asked them to look in their back garden. No Emma there, and their back gate was shut, so she couldn't have escaped that way even if she had made it through the hedge.

I was almost crying by the time Ian walked in.

"I've lost Emma," I said. But I hadn't.

"Look," he said, and there she was, fast asleep, hidden among and dwarfed by her many toys piled in the corner.

I burst into tears of relief. So much for "the sensible route"—fostering a puppy rather than having one of our own. I was already far more attached than I'd thought could be possible.

Soon into the new year, Jack Frost dumped snow all over the East Midlands countryside, and Helper Dog classes were canceled. So, with phone assistance from Jamie and Frank, I began to teach Emma at home.

"How's it going today?" Jamie asked as he picked up the phone to another daily briefing from me.

"Great," I told him, and filled him in on this and that.

"They can be a handful," he said.

I looked down at Emma. I was more than happy to have my hands full with her.

"Make sure you fill in her progress chart and hopefully this snow will clear soon. Any problems give me a call."

Emma was so eager to learn, and my heart melted as I watched her work out what she was supposed to do and tried to do it. I taught her commands for "sit," "down" and "roll over" (but only on the carpet as I didn't want her rolling over on the shiny new—but hard—laminate floor). Jamie advised leaving her collar on at all times so she would just accept wearing it without becoming stressed.

The one thing I wasn't supposed to teach her was how to climb stairs. A little puppy's joints are easily damaged by overstretching, but sometimes a puppy's need to explore takes over, and one day I came out of the kitchen to find her two steps up. Then, the following day, she was five steps toward the sky and attempting the next when I caught her. At the sound of my tutting, however, she stopped and sat there, and it took me a moment to realize that the intrepid puppy, so keen to go up, hadn't the first clue about how to get down again—except by looking plaintive and being lifted down by Mum. As soon as he could, Ian bought a stair gate. Another few pounds to the DIY store; I felt they should be rolling the red carpet out next time we went.

Jamie had explained to me how the puppies were monitored for their suitability for differently abled partners. If the dog has strong joints, it could go to people who needed tasks doing where the dog had to stand on its hind legs a lot. He introduced me to Denise, a lady confined to a wheelchair with limited mobility in her arms, and her dog, Yogi.

"He'd been so well trained that he fitted in with us straightaway," she said, "and ever since the first day I brought him home he's been turning the lights on and off for me. Sometimes if it's cloudy he does it without asking!" She smiled at the recollection. "He also presses the button at the pedestrian crossing, no problem. Before, I had to wait until someone came along and ask them to do it for me. Strangers in the street are always amazed when he does it. It makes me laugh to see their shocked faces. I laugh a lot more now I have him with me. He's so funny."

Yogi put his head on Denise's lap and she stroked him fondly.

Never mind the stairs, Emma still had a long way to go in all aspects of her training. She and I picked our way through the snowy garden—and, when it was blizzarding, around the living room—so that she would become habituated to being on the lead and resist the temptation to chew it. Plus there was the continual toilet training on the bark-chip area. She was pretty much toilet-trained within a week of arriving with us, apart from the odd accident, of course. Often, though, these were my fault for not taking her outside when she was most likely in need. Emma loved the beautiful snowy garden, though I only let her out for short stretches of time as I didn't want her to get too cold.

Helper Dogs insists that puppies are only given one minute's walk for each week of their life, so at eight weeks Emma could have an eight-minute walk—but not on the road or the park or anywhere that a dog who hadn't been vaccinated might have been. We had to keep her under virtual puppy house arrest until she was old enough to have her second round of inoculations. I loved the little puppy-dog sounds she made as she ran across the snowy garden or "talked" to Spiky, who was almost her equal in size. Toys were pounced on with delight and dragged through the snow, and always, as tiny puppies do, she needed to be within a few feet of me. If I moved across the garden, she'd be there next to me in a flash.

When we could, too, we carried her out in a little bag so that she could experience as much of what the world had to offer as possible even before her second vaccination. Cue trips to the supermarket, frosty walks by the river and a bottom-numbing half an hour sitting near one of the local main roads, so that she'd get used to the sound of traffic and become habituated to huge trucks and lorries barreling past—after all, there's no way except experience for a puppy to know that drivers have also been trained, and that they won't mow down passersby. All Helper Dogs must be taught to sit at each curb and wait to be told to cross the road. They also (depending on the needs of the person they're placed with) may be taught to press the button at a pelican crossing to stop the traffic, like Yogi, the dog we'd met who helps Denise. Whenever we left the house, people wanted to say hello to Emma—she was impossible to resist—and she was pleased to have the attention.

Every now and then, I wondered if her mum was missing her. I thought she must be, so I rang the breeders to find out more about Emma's first family. They were very pleased to learn that she'd arrived safely and was eating well.

"Guide Dogs for the Blind have always taken all of the puppies before, but this year they couldn't use them all. We've never had two puppies go to Helper Dogs before," they said. "And she's such a dainty little thing. We'll send you some photos of her mum and the other puppies in the litter."

I reassured them that Ian and I would love and take care of her, and promised to keep in touch and let them know how Emma was progressing.

Finally the snow cleared and Emma and I were able to attend our first Helper Dogs class. There were *ooh*s and begs of *can I have a cuddle* from Stacey and Kate, the two dog groomers who had a salon adjacent to the training center. Emma happily obliged.

"She's just the sweetest thing."

I smiled my agreement.

"Ouch!"

Oh yes, she'd just started doing that. Emma had found her teeth and they could be like little needles.

Emma was overjoyed to see Eddie, her brother. Liz, Eddie's puppy parent, told me that Eddie was also chewing like crazy. Jamie gave us all teething toys.

"Try to distract them with a toy," he said. "It's a stage they all go through, but you don't want them damaging your stuff."

"Or us!" said Jo. She was the third puppy parent to receive a Christmas puppy. Hers was a black Labrador called Elvis who seemed to like nothing more than sleeping in his crate. Eddie, Elvis and Emma. All so named because of their age: Helper Dogs, like many assistance-dogs charities, found it easier for quick reference to name dogs of the same intake with the same letter.

"He just loves his bed," Jo said. "He wakes up in the morning around nine . . ."

Liz and I exchanged a look: sleeping till nine sounded like total luxury.

". . . and then he has his breakfast and a little play and he goes back to bed for an hour—or maybe a little longer. He just takes himself off to sleep. That's when I get my housework done or go grocery shopping."

My eyebrows had almost shot off the top of my head by this juncture. There hadn't been much sleeping—let alone housework—going on in our house, and Ian was picking up ready-meals every night on his way home from work. We didn't want to leave Emma by herself for a second.

"She has to learn to be alone at some point," said a woman in the corner who hadn't spoken before.

"This is Diane," Jamie said. "She's an experienced puppy

parent visiting today from the Peterborough center." Diane had a Labradoodle that was sitting rigidly to attention beside her.

"It's like being a parent," Diane said. She looked over at Liz. "Do you have children?"

"Yes."

"How about you?" She looked over at Jo.

"Grown up now," Jo said. "I'm a granny."

"How about you?" Diane said to me. "Do you have children?"

I hesitated, for fear of stumbling over my words, but Diane didn't wait for my reply. "When you're a parent, you develop a sixth sense of when your kids are up to something. Suddenly you seem to have eyes in the back of your head."

"Hear, hear," laughed Liz. "I need to with my lot."

"And that's why people who've had children make the best puppy parents," Diane announced.

I concentrated on Emma, who was pawing my leg, so Diane wouldn't notice she'd upset me. I might not have had the experience of having children, but I was going to be the very best puppy parent I could be.

"You OK, Megan?" Jamie asked when Diane left shortly afterward.

"Oh, fine," I said, sighing. But I was worried about leaving Emma when I went for my monthly blood test and scan. Sometimes, if there were a lot of people waiting, it could take ages for me to be seen. And, despite what Diane said, I wasn't ready to lock Emma up in the house on her own for hours.

"Pop her around to me," Jo said. "I'm only up the road

from you, and she and Elvis can have a play together."

"It'll be at least every month," I said. "Maybe twice a month sometimes."

"Not a problem at all."

Now that Diane had gone back to Peterborough, I was starting to enjoy the Helper Dogs class and the new friends I was making.

5

Puppies, it was turning out, were a bit of a full-time job. Even without the dozens of trips to the garden in every twenty-four-hour period, there were bundles of forms to fill in, charts to plot, diaries to keep. I felt as if I needed a secretary to keep on top of the admin, while I got on with the important business of loving and caring for Emma. And then there was our first visit to the vet.

Emma had been given her first vaccination before we got her, and she was due a second at ten weeks. Together, the two puppy inoculations protected against some real nasties including canine distemper, viral hepatitis, parvovirus, leptospirosis and other diseases that sounded like you wouldn't wish them on your worst enemy. Even a quick glance at the list of potential symptoms—diarrhea, vomiting, deep hacking coughs, fever, collapse and sometimes death—was almost enough to convince me never to let Emma out of the house without a biohazard suit on. Parvovirus, in particular, I'd heard a lot about as Jamie had been muttering darkly about an outbreak of "parvo" in our area; because of the vaccinations it wasn't very common, so when a dog did catch it the outlook was bad. Puppies, naturally, were particularly vulnerable, and could die within a couple of days due to fluid loss. On top of the vaccinations, Emma would need to be wormed every month for the first six months, but it would be Jamie and Helper Dogs that provided the tablets. Dogs shouldn't have worms for their own health, but the worms' larvae also posed a health risk to people, and young children and babies in particular.

"Don't put her down on the floor," the receptionist said when we signed in at the vet's and she realized how young Emma was. "Not until she's had her second vaccination; you wouldn't want her to catch anything."

No fear.

Nevertheless, Emma was very interested in the much larger and older dogs that came into the vet's. I wasn't sure if she was allowed to say hello to them or not so tried to keep my distance, although Emma really wanted to clamber out of my arms and over to them.

When the vet finally called out "Emma Rix" it gave me a little thrill to hear her name. We went into the treatment room and I put her onto the treatment table.

"Hello," said the vet. "Aren't you lovely?"

She checked Emma over and listened to her heart through a stethoscope. Then she frowned and listened again.

"She's got a bit of a heart murmur," she said.

Our little puppy had a heart murmur. I didn't really know what it meant, but it sounded terrible.

"It might not be bad at all," reassured the vet when she saw panic in my eyes. "Quite often young puppies grow out of them. But we'll have to keep an eye on her. Don't let her get overtired."

She gave Emma her injection and checked the microchip that she'd been given before she came to us, and we were free to go.

I carried Emma out to the car and put her into her crate

in the back. Our little girl had a heart murmur. Please let her be OK, please let her be OK, I kept repeating to myself as I drove home.

I soon got used to the endless rounds of forms, forms and more forms. Every week I had to fill in a progress diary to show how Emma was getting on and to highlight any areas that we needed to concentrate on. These were then collected by Jamie at class each week and forwarded on to the head office.

One of the more fun forms to fill in was the "What has your puppy seen and who has your puppy met?" form. I liked ticking off the boxes.

"Has your puppy seen someone wearing a hat?" Tick.

"Met a baby?" Tick.

"Seen a person with an umbrella?" Tick.

People wearing hats and people carrying umbrellas are often confusing to dogs. A person wearing a hat can suddenly look quite different and someone putting up an umbrella . . . that must look really bizarre to an animal. Other forms asked how well the puppy was eating, if she'd had any tummy upsets or if she'd shown any fear and aggression. Helper Dogs puppies are taught that they must give up their toy on the word "give," with the usual pats and praise when they do. Some dogs growl if an owner goes near their food bowl when they're eating, but aggressive possessiveness is never allowed. We had to be completely sure that everything we did reinforced positive behavior, and that any bad behavior was studiously ignored.

Puppies naturally want to do well and make their owner happy, and good early care will give the dog the temperament and skills it needs for a long and useful life. A Helper

Dog partner can put their absolute trust in their dog, expect their behavior to be excellent and for them to adjust to all sorts of situations. When the Helper Dog first comes into the disabled person's family, only the person they're partnered with feeds, grooms and exercises them, to strengthen the bond between them. I met Vicky, a Helper Dog partner, at the center one day, and over the months we became friends, often chatting after Emma's class. Vicky was a bright, bubbly eighteen-year-old who'd been knocked off her bike by a speeding driver when she was twelve and left fighting for her life in the hospital. After months of operations, grafts and intensive rehabilitation, Vicky and her family had been told to face up to the fact that Vicky would need to use a wheelchair and would require care and twenty-four-hour supervision for the rest of her life.

"Before I had my Helper Dog, Whoopi," she said, "it was always me that other people were doing things for. If I dropped something, I had to wait till someone picked it up for me. When it was my birthday, I couldn't even pick up my own birthday cards off the mat and had to wait for my mum to come back from the shops and give them to me. My mum didn't feel like she could leave me alone in the house for more than an hour, in case something happened or I needed even something minor done for me.

"When I got Whoopi, Helper Dogs told me that she was my dog and my responsibility—not my mum's or anyone else's. If I didn't give Whoopi her food and water, then Whoopi would be hungry and thirsty. If I didn't groom her, then her coat would get all matted and if I didn't take her for a walk then she wouldn't get a walk—and Whoopi loves walks, she really really loves them! It was a lot of work at first, which I wasn't used to doing, but eventually it started to make me so happy to take care of her, and I started becoming more active and taking pride in things again. And she does a thousand times more things for me than I could ever do for her. Every day I do everything I can for Whoopi and every day she does everything and more for me. Some things I don't even ask her to do—like she'll push the footplate on my wheelchair down for me and put the pillow back on my bed if it falls off. She's my very best friend in the whole world."

Still, the puppy progress forms seemed to take up a lot of time, especially as I tried to use the space for comments and requests to give as much helpful information as possible. Jamie also suggested including a photo or two of her. I told him about the blog Ian had set up for Emma the day after we'd got her, in which we wrote a little diary, explaining how the world looked from a puppy's point of view—what she'd seen, what she'd learned and how she felt about her new puppy parents. It was fun to write; Ian had even taken a photo of tiny Emma at a laptop, to go at the top.

Ten days after her vaccination, Emma was able to go for her first proper walk down by the river. The long, damp grass excited her and she sniffed at everything, encountering a thousand new smells, tastes and sensations for the very first time. But back home after our short (ten-minute) walk she started crying, rubbing her paws on the carpet and running to me for help.

Somewhere close to home, she'd run through a patch of stinging nettles and discovered for the first time that there

was bad as well as good out there in the world. Her tender baby's paws were stung and she didn't know what to do. Ian and I didn't know what to do either and were almost as panicked as she was. She needed us to help, but we weren't doing our jobs, we weren't being proper puppy parents. We put her in a bath and the water soothed a little, but then the stinging came back and she started crying again.

I phoned Helper Dogs, but Jamie wasn't there, so I made my way down the list of volunteers' numbers until finally Julia answered: "Put some Savlon on," she said. "Their little paws are very sensitive. If you have any baby socks, put them over the Savlon so she doesn't lick it off and make herself sick."

But by the time I got off the phone, the stinging had worn off and Emma was having a cuddle on the sofa with Ian.

"Poor little puppy girl," he said.

And Emma did look like she was feeling very sorry for herself. I sat down next to her on the sofa and she crawled over to me and buried herself in my lap. When somehow she managed to force down a little treat Ian offered her and then looked up hopefully for another one, we knew she must be OK.

I felt lucky that I knew the other Helper Dogs puppy parents, all of whom I could count on and trust, and who were far more experienced than me with puppies. I also realized that I was counting on them increasingly for companionship and counting on them as friends too. The Helper Dogs volunteers and all the other dog walkers at the river were making me feel at home in the village for the first time. Initially, I'd felt isolated and hated it. I missed my friends and my family who were all back in London. Ian worked such long hours and sometimes I didn't see anyone besides him from one day to the next. There were no other writers or writers' groups anywhere near, and when I told people what I did for a living, they reacted like I was an odd, exotic butterfly, a specimen to be examined but not quite trusted.

When we first decided to get married, we'd talked about moving to the south coast, but that idea had never really taken flight. Ian came from a family that, once they'd bought a house, seemed to live there for the rest of their lives, sometimes generations. I couldn't understand it, but because he was bringing home most of the money and working such long hours to provide a home for us, I didn't like to be too grumpy about it. I consoled myself by making our house look as nice as it could. At least then it'd be ready to be sold when he was ready to move.

Now, though, I was firmly embedded within the dog-walking community. Ian's choice of home seemed perfect and I didn't have time to think about moving. There were Jenny and Karen with their dog, Butch, and Mike with his dog, Trudy. Liz and Eddie lived only a mile away, and Jo and Elvis and Len and Daisy were even closer, so we started to arrange to meet up once a week or so. And, even when I didn't make special arrangements, I knew that at just about any time of day, every single day, all I had to do was step out to the river and I'd find some fellow dog walkers with whom to laugh, chat or moan, a little community united by our dogs.

Everyone reacted differently toward me now that I had a puppy. They were much, much friendlier and were always stopping to talk. Even the postman, who I used to just smile and nod to, would now make a second trip to our house if I wasn't in because he knew I'd probably just popped out for a walk with Emma and would be back soon.

Each week Emma's walk got a little longer, until we finally made it all the way down the river path to the meadow for the first time—an open, flat piece of land, which in the summer would be filled with flowers and walkers, but in February was the sole preserve of dog-lovers and canine types. There we met an elderly lady called Florence with three elderly dogs—Brutus, a German Shepherd, and Cleo and Caesar, two small mongrels. Emma tried to play with them, but they weren't interested in playing with an exuberant puppy. It's hard for puppies to understand that older dogs don't always want to play. I didn't trust the German Shepherd much, even though I knew that when he barked at her all he really meant was "Back off, young un!" I told Florence how we'd be keeping Emma for about six months, and then she'd be leaving us to continue with the next stage of her training. Usually when I said this, the other person would sympathize: *It's going to be so hard to give her up*, they'd say. *I know, I know* was my stock response.

Although, of course, I didn't really know anything about it, as I'd never had to give a puppy up before.

I told Florence that eventually Emma would be going to help a disabled person.

"That's terrible," she said.

"Pardon?"

"It's not much of a life for a dog, is it, stuck inside all the time. Her keeper's not going to be able to take her out for a walk like this." She opened her arms wide to indicate the meadow and the wooded area. It stretched for miles with the river running along beside it.

No, I supposed they wouldn't, and I didn't have a ready reply.

I asked Jamie about it.

"The dogs don't go to just anyone who wants them," he said. "The person has to live in a place with a garden and the dog must be able to be taken for walks. Usually there are friends and family to help with the walking too. And the dog is checked up on regularly. We have people whose job is to provide the after-care and to check up on the dogs and to remove them if everything isn't OK."

I couldn't forget what Florence had said. I already had a small inkling of the wrench it would be to give Emma up, and I knew that it would break my heart twice over if I wasn't totally convinced she was going on to the best life possible for her. I wanted Emma to have walks and fun, and not just work all the time. I simply wouldn't be able to let her go, if that was the case, and began dreading the day I'd be asked to do so.

6

Emma barked as the doorbell rang. She was always excited to have visitors; all guests, in her mind, came solely to see her.

"We've got news!" my brother, Jack, had said to me on the phone, but he'd refused to go into any more detail without being face-to-face. So here he was, with his girlfriend, Carmel, on a rare visit.

He walked in, full of pent-up energy, barely able to contain himself, pecking me on the cheek as he thundered past down the hall and into the living room; Carmel looked pleased. Barely were they inside and the kettle on than it exploded out of him.

"Carmel's pregnant!"

Carmel beamed with delight and out poured the story of how this had happened. I kept a smile on my face and hoped no one would notice that I was in shock. Of course I was pleased for them, but I was jealous too.

When Jack and Carmel had moved in together, more than five years previously, they hadn't mentioned wanting to have a baby. I'd had no idea whatsoever that it was part of their plans, although, given he was now forty years old and she forty-three, I'd perhaps been naive in thinking it wasn't on the agenda. It was just something that in our family we didn't seem to think about—in the same way that, before I'd met Ian, I'd been happily without kids myself.

Carmel had talked to me once or twice over the years about having fibroids, but fibroids were a nuisance—and sometimes plenty more than that—to many women, regardless of whether they were trying to conceive.

Now, clasping hands on the sofa, they revealed that they'd been trying for a baby for years and had been living the agony of not being able to conceive alone, without telling anyone at all, even their nearest and dearest. Carmel had undergone more than one operation, and they'd had repeated IVF treatments without success. Only a few months previously, their specialist had warned that it was highly unlikely ever to happen, at which news Jack suggested they abandon the treatments, and Carmel agreed, though it broke her heart to do so.

"I used to hate tea before I got pregnant, but now I can't stop drinking it," Carmel said, looking flushed with health as she sipped at her mug and devoured the cake I'd laid on. She carried on with her story.

"And it was only a week or two later that I started to feel a bit funny. I wasn't sick, not vomiting, but I was feeling a bit off. I wasn't myself. All the way to the chemist's, I was telling myself I was being stupid, but I went and did it anyway. I went and bought a pregnancy test, without telling Jack because he would have said I was just wasting money." She gave him a rueful look.

"So I took the test and there was the faintest of positive lines. You had to look really closely to see it. But it was there.

"And so I went to my doctor and told him and do you know what he did?"

We shook our heads. Emma showed Jack her latest toy.

"He shook his head like I was mad and said it was sometimes very hard for women like me to accept that they couldn't get pregnant. And maybe he should refer me for counseling!"

Jack and Carmel laughed. I didn't know what to say.

"But I was pregnant—three months pregnant—and he was wrong! And then I was worried because if I'd known I was pregnant—really pregnant—I'd never have been drinking wine and I hadn't been having the extra folic acid you're supposed to . . ." She bit her lip, concerned. "The fibroids are still inside me, but when they did the scan they said the baby had somehow managed to find a place in between them and is growing fine . . ."

"It's a miracle," Jack said.

"Yes," Carmel agreed.

"I'm so pleased for you," I said.

"What fantastic news," said Ian.

I lay in bed that night asking myself why I hadn't opened up to them then about our anguish. Ian was fast asleep beside me, catching Zs before his early train, but I couldn't let the day go. There had been ample opportunity for me to talk to Jack, and I'd seen Ian look across at me meaningfully, over the table crowded with mugs, cake and the teapot, but he'd kept mum, leaving it to me to broach the subject with my relatives. Perhaps I'd been too stunned, or I'd obscurely felt that to let the secret out would decrease the chances of the magic working. So I hadn't said anything, although I knew that I should have. Why hadn't I said something?

Ian started to snore softly. I stared up at the ceiling,

unable to sleep. Downstairs in her crate Emma made a sound and I went to see her.

"Hello, little girl," I said.

She wagged her tail as I opened the door and trotted out into the garden after me.

I couldn't get Jack and Carmel out of my mind. It felt like an opportunity had passed to share our burden. I was genuinely pleased for them, and, after all, it offered up grounds for hope for Ian and me. If she could get pregnant with all her fertility problems, then surely I could.

"Please let it be our turn next," I whispered. "Oh, please let it be our turn soon."

We were doing everything we could. I'd been taking some herbs, agnus castus and black cohosh, which were recommended on the Internet, and had changed my diet to take in more foods rich in folic acid, like asparagus. I'd also contacted a charity called Baby Makers, who support people having difficulty getting pregnant, on the advice of a friend, Sam, who had finally conceived with their help. Sam had taken a lot of advice from what they called their Pre-conception Program on food and supplements, and had undergone hair analysis to see if she had the right nutrients to enhance her fertility and promote the growth of a baby. It also showed if there was too much of a mineral or metal that would harm her chances. Sam also enjoyed their newsletter, which featured many people who'd successfully had babies against the odds.

I rang them up and spoke to a lovely lady called Sarah, and finally decided to have the hair analysis myself. It was expensive—causing Ian to mutter that it was a waste of time—but I was willing to give anything a try, from acupuncture to consulting the zodiac, so I chopped a couple of inches off the edge of my thatch and sent it off in the post. How could it hurt? I reasoned. We needed all the help we could get; we'd even raised the end of the bed a few inches, to give gravity a boost.

Jamie was sweeping the doorstep as we drew into the Helper Dogs car park early the next day. It was a bright, cold February morning and, squinting against the low sun, he recognized my car, gave a wave and then creased up with laughter. I got out and, rather defensively, suspecting I had biro on my face or something, asked what the joke was.

"It's not you," he managed before composing himself. "It's the little princess."

He pointed to Emma, who was sitting on her new car seat, resplendent in her new harness. We'd got frustrated with always putting her in her crate for car journeys. It was cumbersome and it didn't allow her the freedom to enjoy the view, which seemed to me like a bad idea when she was supposed to be experiencing as much as possible. First, we found her a car harness in the pet shop, so she'd be safe; then, in a motoring shop, we saw a pink bolster seat with a crown and "Little Princess on Board" written on the cover—and so we'd bought that too.

"Only you could get her something like that!" laughed Jamie.

I didn't see what was so funny. The car seat seemed perfect to me. Now Emma could sit in the passenger seat and look out of the window.

*

Jamie came up to me after the class as I finished chatting with Liz.

"About the blog you and Ian have been doing . . ." he said. "Well, I had a look at it and I think it's great. Do you think you might be able to write it up as a column in the local newspaper?"

Why not? We were writing about puppy life from Emma's point of view, and the blog had become a hit with our friends. I was sure other people would like to read about all the trouble she had training her wayward puppy parents.

A chorus of *oooh*s and *ahhh*s and *isn't it sweet*s greeted us as we walked across the tatty carpet tiles in the newsroom foyer. We went up to the front desk.

"Hi, I'm here to see Jill Bryson—for the animal page," I told the receptionist.

She rang through as we sat down.

"She's lovely," the receptionist said, coming out from behind her desk as Jill and some other journalists from the newspaper came down. Everyone made a big fuss of Emma, who looked gorgeous, behaved impeccably and managed not to pee anywhere or on anyone in all the excitement.

"We'd love you to do a newspaper column about her," Jill said.

"I was thinking of doing the column from Emma's point of view—what it's like living with us and that sort of thing," I explained.

"Sounds good—look forward to reading it."

"How long? How long do you want it to be?"

"Oh, about five hundred words, maybe eight hundred."

Every week? I hoped I'd have enough to write about.

"And photos—we'll need a photo with her column each week." That wasn't a problem. The first one would be of Emma sitting at the keyboard, tapping the keys and getting her dispatch to the editor, eager to start the presses on the next day's edition.

Ian came home to champagne.

"Our little girl's got her own newspaper column. She's going to be famous!" I said as we clinked glasses. "But we need to have a new photo of her every week. We'll need to take her to some interesting places."

Emma really seemed to have brought lots of reasons to celebrate into our lives. I phoned Jamie and he was delighted.

"Maybe it'll help recruit some more volunteers," he said. Helper Dogs always needed more volunteers.

For the first week I wrote about how I felt when I first met her, alongside Emma's diary, which recounted the events from the eyes of a seven-week-old pup. Ian helped with the writing and we took hundreds of photos of Emma doing lots of things, which the newspaper used to accompany the articles each week.

WEDNESDAY: FIRST DAY

Still a little sleepy today. I've just arrived at my new parents' house after a very long journey. They are a nice couple called Meg and Ian. They gave me lots of toys to play with and luckily don't seem to mind if I make a little mess in the house. They keep putting me on some bark chips in the garden. I like chewing them.

THURSDAY: TRAINING CLASS

Meg took me to the Helper Dogs class this morning. I was so sleepy because Meg and Ian kept me up all night wanting to go out to the bark-chip area. I wouldn't mind, but they never seemed to do anything when they got there. I met my brother Eddie at the class and we had a nice play together and he told me about the people he's with—they kept him up all night too!

WEEKEND: TRAINING IAN

Ian's training is coming along well—although he keeps saying "Shake hands" for no reason. I've found that if I wave my paw at him when he says this he sometimes stops. They also keep asking me to sit—can't they see I'm much too busy to sit down?

MONDAY: TOYS

Meg put my toys in something called a washing machine and they spun round and round. I didn't like it. I was worried about my favorite toy Spiky—I like to cuddle up to him at night and carry him around by his ear.

WEDNESDAY: ELVIS

I went to play with another Helper Dogs puppy today. His name's Elvis. He's a little black Labrador. Elvis loves sleeping even more than me. I tried to show Elvis how my mum carried me by the scruff of my neck when I was a baby, but Elvis didn't like it.

Jamie said the piece made him cry, which I took to be a vote of endorsement, but the newspaper found it too long and cut it mercilessly—so much that it may as well have been written by a dog, for all the sense it made. I felt I'd let Emma down and from then on always came in bang on my word limit, so they'd have as little justification to cut as possible.

Emma was much keener on traveling in the car now that she had a car harness and could sit in the front seat. So I arranged one day to meet Eddie, Elvis, Liz and Jo at a country park. Waiting at one set of lights, the man in the car next to us rolled his window down and asked if he could buy Emma from me. I told him I wouldn't sell her for any price, but as I drove on a little voice at the back of my head kept on repeating that Emma would be leaving me, whether I wanted her to or not. When she'd arrived, six months had seemed a long time, but, in the whirlwind of new duties and watching her grow, two months had passed in a flash. With every walk, every game and every bark, the day was coming closer. I turned on the radio and pushed the thought aside. It was too horrible to think about.

Emma was over the moon to see Eddie and Elvis. She loved to scrap with her brother while Elvis looked on, bemused. She'd recently worked out that if she grabbed hold of another puppy's collar with her teeth then the other puppy had to go where she wanted. Eddie was too fast and too wise to fall for this more than a few times, but she managed to hoodwink Elvis all afternoon. The park had a shallow lake that was perfect for dogs to paddle and swim in. Emma was having a lot of fun splashing around with Elvis (who loved any water and once ran under a Great

Dane, so he could be showered with wee) and then suddenly started paddling. She was swimming!

"Emma's had her first swim!" I excitedly told Ian on the phone.

Jamie wasn't quite so impressed.

Swimming isn't advised as a regular activity as it may be hard for some disabled people to dry the dog off afterward, although it is good for the dog to be at home in the water. More than one Helper Dog has saved its owner from drowning, and one I heard of, Waldo, even pulled his owner, Gary, from the shower floor when Gary had a fit and fell unconscious. He then put Gary into the recovery position, covered him with a blanket and ran to a neighbor's house to get help.

To celebrate her newspaper column and first swim, we took Emma to the pet shop to choose a new toy. Not that she needed any more: she now had two toy boxes, both pretty full. Ian loved buying things for her and rarely came home without something for Emma or me. He really was the best present buyer in the world, and he'd absolutely fallen for our little furball too. We hadn't really talked about what it would be like to give her up, and as much as I was delighted that he loved her as much as I did, I also worried, late at night when trudging around the garden with the little one, that we were both falling head over heels without thinking about the inevitable heartbreak that was drawing inexorably closer.

At the pet shop Emma chose three toys: a red dinosaur, a snake rattler and a sheep. Later on, still shopping, I gave

Emma the new rattlesnake to play with and a man came over to make a fuss of her. He took the snake and let her chase it, then tried to trick her by hiding it behind his back.

"Where is it? Where is it?" he said, moving the toy from hand to hand behind his back.

Emma gave him a considering look, buried her head into the bag of new toys, pulled out the red dinosaur and started playing with that instead.

7

Jo proved to be as good as her word and took Emma in whenever I needed a bit of time to go to the hospital. It meant I didn't have to worry when the appointment inevitably took longer than I'd hoped, and she didn't mind if I arrived back, as I did one afternoon, a little upset and needing a cup of tea.

"All right?" she asked.

I shook my head. It wasn't going well. I was very aware of the internal cogs creaking and the second hand ticking by on my poor old biological clock, and it felt like I was wasting the little time I had left—I was realistic that it wasn't much. Maybe if we'd opted to go private and been seen quicker, I'd be pregnant by now. Everything had gone smoothly for the first few months on Clomid, but now my monthly cycles were anything but, and I was bleeding midway through as well. It was like my body was in revolt, doing everything it could to stop me from having any chance of getting pregnant at all.

"My daughter had to wait five years between her three," Jo said, as I told her all this and dried my eyes. "They thought they'd never be able to have another one, and then they had twins. Your turn will come."

But it was hard to find consolation after the monthly poking and prodding. I looked over at Emma, who was curled up asleep with Elvis next to a larger-than-puppy-

68

size toy giraffe, and my heart lifted a little. I woke the little bundle up, strapped her on to her pink princess seat and took her home.

Mum was on the phone.

"Your dad and I have sold Gran's flat," she said.

When my grandmother died, they'd decided to rent her flat out. It was a nice upstairs maisonette in London, with views from the bedroom toward the Thames, and given that I was looking for somewhere to live at the time, we decided that I should rent it from them. I'd lived a metropolitan life in Gran's flat for more than five years before I met Ian, never imagining that one day I could be happy in the sticks, walking beside another river, seeing kingfishers and swans, herons and deer, with a beautiful puppy at my side.

I heard some commotion in the background, and then Dad took the phone from Mum.

"Listen, love, we wanted to help you out a bit, so there's a check in the post for you." He paused. "It's for ten thousand pounds."

Once I got over the shock I kept the news close to me like a treasured secret all day. My mind was racing, and I couldn't help but think of a thousand—ten thousand— things to do with the money, but first I had to talk to Ian. We discussed it that night over dinner.

"What do you think your gran would have wanted you to spend it on?" he asked.

I shrugged. "Gran just always wanted her grandchildren to be happy."

"Do you think she would have liked a great-grandchild?"

"Oh yes—she'd have loved to have one."

Ian stroked my hair and said softly, "I think we should spend the money on a private fertility clinic."

"Do you really?"

Ian nodded and my heart lifted for the first time in a week. Maybe a private clinic would be the answer. We'd told the specialist, Mrs. Hughes, we didn't want to go down the IVF route, and it wasn't available to us on the NHS because of my age, but now it seemed more and more like a sensible option to explore, and I was sure it would be available privately.

And so we decided that was what we would do.

The weather now was warm enough to start dreaming of summer, and we began to talk about how much Emma would like to go to the seaside. Ian found a great holiday cottage—one of six—on a dog-friendly farm near the sea in East Anglia and booked a long weekend, as he could only get a few days off work. I drove Emma down during the day and we arrived in time to pick him up as his train piled into the small Suffolk station.

The cottage was beautiful, although much smaller than it looked in the glossy brochure. From the very center of the living room, a twisting wrought-iron spiral staircase led up to a four-poster bed nestled among the eaves. Quite predictably, Emma went straight for the staircase—the only thing I wanted to forbid her—so I took her out for a walk around the farm to tire her out while Ian got us settled in and made some phone calls. It was rare that he could take time completely off from the office.

On our stroll, Emma and I discovered there weren't

actually many animals on the farm. A couple of chickens scratching around by the farmhouse kitchen, some dogs and some ducks on the pond. I wasn't sure what Emma would have made of anything larger or wilder than another dog, and she'd seen ducks already on the river at home. It was nice to see, however, that she got on well with the other dogs, as I'd been making the effort to socialize her. A homely smell of cooking greeted me as we returned; Ian was in the kitchen, with the back doors open on to our own little deck, which was encircled by a sturdy, Emma-proof fence and had a hot tub in the corner. Really, the cottage was perfect for us. Ian cracked open a bottle of wine, and with Emma now asleep on the deck beside us, we tried out the hot tub as we waited for the stew to stew.

At bedtime I put the suitcase in front of the spiral staircase so Emma wouldn't try to come up. She was exhausted, and we'd been hoping she'd implicitly understand the concept of "holiday" and have a little lie-in, but although we didn't hear a peep from her all night, it wasn't to be. She woke as usual at 5 a.m.—either because she wanted to help Ian with his morning commuter routine or because of the cocks' untimely crowing, I didn't know—and Ian obligingly went downstairs to let her outside. No sooner had he moved the suitcase and turned his back to put the kettle on, than she was up the spiral staircase to find me. Conclusively proving that a four-month-old puppy is more energetic than two fully grown adults, she was at the top before he could do anything. She jumped on the bed, extremely proud of herself, waking me from my doze.

"Morning, Emma," I said, from a warm, dream-clouded

place. "How nice and still she is," I thought abstractly from my fug; it was unusual for Emma to keep so still. The bed was very comfortable, so maybe I'd even snatch a few more minutes' sleep . . . then I felt a warm spreading feeling on my legs and realized what had happened.

"Emma's weed on the bed!" I shouted.

Ian raced up the stairs. Our accommodation might have been dog friendly, but that didn't mean they wanted dogs on the beds and it certainly didn't mean they wanted puppies having accidents on them. It was barely light outside, but the cockerels were getting more persistent.

"Quick!" Ian said, leaping around the bed with his dressing gown flapping. We had stripped the sheets, washed the quilt and cover in the laundry room and festooned the insides of our tiny cottage with large sheets hung up to dry before anyone else was up.

Emma loved the seaside even more than we'd hoped she would. The Suffolk waves were gentle, and once she'd got over the idea of a limitless expanse of water, she liked running in and out of them, snapping at them and then rolling in the sand. It was the sand she liked best; it awoke within her an urge to dig, dig, dig, down and down, until she'd created a hole bigger than herself—which she then dived into and in which she became half buried when, in trying to get out, one of the walls caved in under her scrabbling paws.

A minute later, barely recovered, she spotted a man about to go for a paddle, sitting on his towel having removed his shoes. She yelped and ran over and started attempting to pull his socks off for him.

"What's she doing?" he laughed (fortunately he wasn't dog-phobic). We told him about Helper Dogs. She'd been doing what she'd been taught to do but had forgotten that she was supposed to wait to be asked to do it! Bidding him and his socks goodbye, we retired from the beach to a café and thence back home, where Emma collapsed in a sandy little heap, exhausted once more, and we enjoyed another evening surrounded by cock-crows and the dark, flat Suffolk countryside.

Helper Dogs didn't just help their partners at work; I'd heard many stories about how they'd improved their quality of life by enabling their owners to go on holiday, sometimes for the first time. A very calm black Labrador I met called Annie had an eight-year-old partner, Paul, who had autism and didn't speak.

"We've had our first family holiday ever thanks to Annie," said Leila, Paul's mother. "It would have been too stressful and too much for Paul to handle before. But she has such a calming influence on him. Plus, because of her special harness that's attached to Paul around his waist, I don't have to worry if Paul gets freaked out by something and tries to run off. Annie just sits down and Paul comes to a stop, and often sits down too!

"I thought Paul would be really freaked out by his first sight of the sea, but he wasn't—just kept staring at it. He didn't like the ice-cream van, though," she said, laughing at the memory. "Also, having Annie with us with her assistance dog coat on means when Paul has a tantrum, when it all gets too much for him, people realize he isn't just being a naughty boy with a mum that's spoilt him! We were very lucky: Helper Dogs don't often train dogs to work with children like Paul—although there are some charities that specialize in it."

Though my weekend with Emma and Ian was all too short, the break did us a world of good. Ian had had a few days away from the London commute, Emma had seen the sea for the first time and I'd barely thought about Clomid once. I came home refreshed and remembered that the £10,000 had cleared into my savings account.

The following week, I spent hours on the computer browsing the many Internet forums in which women described their experiences of trying to have children. I especially liked looking at the ones for older women who'd successfully become pregnant. Then I researched the private clinics within driving distance from us: some didn't offer IVF for women over forty; some only offered donor eggs. But there were two that looked right.

I explored all the possibilities the money gave us in my mind and began to come to some decisions. I e-mailed both clinics and asked to be sent more details.

8

Emma's head was deep inside the washing machine, and I loved it. I'd been cultivating this behavior, egging her on with praise and treats for days. First I'd used a favorite toy, placing it right on the edge of the machine, and showered her with love when she brought it back to me. Gradually I'd put it farther and farther inside, until she had her head completely within the dark echoey drum; her tail, which was sticking right out into the kitchen, was swishing merrily from side to side like a metronome, marking how happy she was.

It was one of the many skills that all Helper Dogs had to learn. For an able-bodied person, taking the washing out of the machine is simply a tiresome chore, but in a wheelchair or with limited mobility, it can be a struggle. Now, after only a couple of weeks' practice, Emma was cheerfully—and surprisingly delicately—pulling socks, pants and bras out with her mouth and dropping them into the washing basket, ready to be taken outside to be hung up to dry. It was a game to her, one she loved to play.

Learning how to take the pegs from the basket and give them to me, however, was all her own work. After the washing-machine drill, she followed me out into the garden and, in an excess of play-fever, simply copied what I was doing. Soon, I'd say, "Peg, Emma," and she'd bring me a peg over; and when I was unpegging the washing, she could take the pegs gently from my hand and drop them back into the basket too. For her, it was a fun, exciting game, well rewarded with treats and love..Someday, the washing-machine game and the peg game would make somebody's life a whole lot easier. She was really picking up new skills quickly now; most of all, she was enjoying it.

Other things we concentrated on were taking off a person's shoes and socks, picking up a dropped walking stick and finding the phone—what's a few tooth marks on a phone if it means your dog can bring it to you when you've had a nasty fall and need help? She was also very good at finding a set of door keys to which I'd attached a cuddly toy keyring. "Find the keys," I'd say, and off she'd go, hunting around the room. Sometimes, I'd hide them in a shoe or under a cushion so she really had to look for them. Sometimes I even buried them inside a pile of her toys. She never gave up until she found them and she always had a treat and tons of happy praise when she brought them over. I was certain that a huge smile spread over her doggy face every time.

Quite aside from the specialized Helper Dogs work, Emma was coming on in leaps and bounds in her obedience training. All Helper Dogs had to complete Kennel Club training, too, as it was equally as important to their prospective partners that they could do simple things such as stay and sit on command as it was that they'd perform the more complicated tasks. Jamie had decided that it was time for Emma and Eddie to go for their first Kennel Club exam. Elvis hadn't yet quite grasped what was required of him and was going to wait until later when his behavior was less erratic.

Ted, a man in his thirties with cerebral palsy, told me how his working day had changed after his Helper Dog, Callum, came to live with him. At first Ted had thought that Callum's most important skill was being as quiet and unobtrusive as possible; however, he soon found out that there were much bigger benefits than that.

"At work I never used to speak to anyone if I could help it and no one ever spoke to me. Some days I'd go through a whole day sitting at my computer without saying anything. Around me other people in the office would be chatting, but not me. I was the invisible man—there but not there. When I got Callum and took him to work, it was like people saw Ted the person for the first time. Everyone wanted to say hello to Callum and ask questions about him. Soon it took me ten minutes to get to my desk because everyone wanted to stop and say hello.

"Callum is really good and sits under my desk. He's not in the way at the office at all. Now, when it's lunch hour, a group of us from the office take Callum to the park so he can have a run around and sometimes we even go to the pub after work. I just have orange juice—don't want to be drunk in charge of a wheelchair!"

Knowing how important it was for Emma to be obedient didn't make me any more relaxed, and on the day of the exam, I struggled to control my nerves. I didn't want to affect her performance. Eight or ten other dogs—Helper Dogs and dogs from the normal obedience classes—lined up across the lawn, and one by one they were put through their paces. Emma walked smartly with her lead, not pulling or lagging behind, and returned straightaway when she was

77

called. There remained one final test: she had to lie still in one place for a minute while I walked away. As I patted and praised her, she settled into the down position well. I commanded her to stay. She lay still, perfectly obedient, until the time was up, but as I came back to her, she sat up—and, by so doing, failed the test. It was such a shame that she'd fallen at the final hurdle, but she wasn't to know that she'd done anything wrong, so I gave her a piece of cheese as a reward anyway. She'd have a chance to retake it in a month's time. Eddie passed without a problem.

Not all dogs are as well behaved, as we found out soon after on a walk on the riverbank. Emma was now four months old, and although she was growing fast, people recognized her all the time as the puppy in the newspaper column. She took to celebrity well and always welcomed being stroked. I was happy to let people fuss her: it filled me with pride and it was also important that Helper Dogs become used to dealing with the public in all kinds of situations. Passersby and dog walkers always made kind remarks—"It's the best bit in the paper. I always turn to your column first," or "That time she chewed up the toilet rolls . . . But it looks like butter wouldn't melt!"

It made me so happy that people could see how special and lovable she was.

Emma usually got on as swimmingly with dogs as she did with people, but as I was to learn, there are always exceptions. In the weak March sunshine that morning, we met an elderly man and his wife walking a large greyhound. He was a rescue dog, thin and jumpy, and he'd only been with them for a few weeks. While his wife held on to the greyhound, the man stiffly bent down and made a big fuss of Emma. The greyhound looked unhappy enough at this, but when his owner reached into his pocket and gave Emma a biscuit, the larger dog rushed over and bit her. Emma squeaked in shock and pain while the woman pulled the vexed greyhound away.

"She's OK, she's OK," the man said. "It didn't break the skin."

"He was probably just jealous," explained his wife. I could see how a celebrity puppy grabbing all of his owners' attention could make a rescue dog insecure and want to bite, but it didn't really make things any better. It was the first time I'd had to deal with this kind of situation, and I, too, was in shock. Still, I reasoned, Emma didn't seem to be hurt, so I bade them a frosty goodbye and carried on with our walk.

Emma slept as usual when we got back but woke up crying and limping. In a panic, I phoned Jamie, but there was no answer. The organization paid the bills, so we were meant to check with the Helper Dogs bosses before we went to the vet's. But my puppy was hurt, and I wasn't in any mood to hang about. I took her anyway. By the time we got there, she had staged a marvelous recovery and wasn't crying or limping. She licked the vet's face as he tried to examine her. The vet, the receptionist and the whole waiting room were smitten.

"I don't think there's much wrong with this little girl," he said, laughing. "She might have woken up and remembered what had happened. It probably gave her a scare more than anything."

As any mother would be, I was still worried.

"I'll give her an analgesic if it'll make you feel happier."

It certainly did. I also got him to check her heart and was over the moon when he said Emma's heart murmur had disappeared of its own accord.

If only medical problems in my life were so easily resolved. All the tests and (seemingly) inevitable disappointments were getting me down almost as much as being childless. In despair, I confided in Lorrie, a new Helper Dogs volunteer, who was a retired midwife. Lorrie had worked with my specialist, Mrs. Hughes, in the past, and although Lorrie said she had the greatest professional respect for her, she frowned upon hearing that my next appointment was in six months' time. She quickly became as determined as I was that I get pregnant as soon as possible.

"Goodness gracious, woman, you can't wait that long! Write the lady a letter," she said. "If you send a letter, then she'll be obliged to answer you in writing."

I took her advice and wrote, reminding Mrs. Hughes of my test results (poor), my age (advancing) and her decision (Clomid for a year).

I'm writing to you because I am now really desperate to have a baby and am thinking about trying IVF. I believe I would need to do this privately because of my age and was wondering what your advice would be. The private IVF clinic in Billingsford seems to have a good reputation and would currently be my first choice. But I am not sure if IVF should be my next step.

I licked and stamped the envelope, and put it in the post feeling a little as if I'd stoppered up all my hopes and fears and tossed them out to sea in a bottle, with little prospect of ever hearing back. Nevertheless, even having put every-thing down in writing seemed to have lightened the load a little, and I was delighted when a few weeks later I received a reply from Mrs. Hughes speaking positively of the Bill-ingsford clinic. She also took the step of contacting them for me, as well as writing a letter to my local practice, explaining my situation.

My regular doctor had left and I was given a new GP, a registrar called Amy Boston. Her sympathetic manner put me at ease right away when we met, and I opened my heart to her. Dr. Boston reiterated that the NHS did not pay for IVF for women of my age, simply because the results were usually very poor. However, if I decided to go ahead, she would recommend the Billingsford clinic and would forward all my clinical notes to them. Before leaving, I asked her if I could have two blood tests: for FSH (a hormone that encourages eggs to grow) and for LH (one of the most important hormones involved in pregnancy). My last FSH test had been in February, when I'd had a reading of 11.6. This was the same as the previous November, and the range of normal readings went up to 12—so I'd just squeaked inside. Dr. Boston wasn't too worried about this. She printed out a form for me to take to the hospital for my blood test.

After giving Emma her lunch and settling her down, I left for the hospital, feeling much more positive than I had in months. I found a good spot in the hospital car park and went up to the all-too-familiar, all-too-crowded waiting room. The ticket machine spewed out a number—99. It was going to be a long wait.

I sighed and stared down at my tummy. Ian and I had put on a lot of weight since getting together. In fact, I thought, I looked so fat that people must think I'm pregnant already. The flab seemed to gather high up, under my bust, although it was likely that it was evenly spread and just bulged upward when I sat down. Looking at it, I really wished I were pregnant. I wanted it so badly. When 99 finally flashed up, I picked up my handbag and went in to greet the nurses who ran the clinic. It seemed to take ages for enough blood to fill the test tube to come out, and it hadn't got any less painful than last time, but, at last, it was over, and the nurse who'd taken the blood told me to expect the results at my GP's by the following Thursday.

The results, when they came through, were not good.

"There, there, it's all right, don't cry," Dr. Boston said as she handed me tissues number three, four, five and six.

But I couldn't help it.

"It's just I was . . . I was . . . so hoping," I sobbed. "It's not like . . . I'm very happy, I have a lovely husband, a cute puppy, you should see her. Only I'd have liked . . ."

Dr Boston nodded and took my hand. "Maybe you should contact that IVF clinic sooner rather than later," she said.

9

My relationship with Queenie, Jamie's pet German Shepherd, consisted of me avoiding her and her ignoring me and, so far, this had worked out well for both of us. Queenie was the alpha dog of the group: huge, and with her long glossy coat, every inch the queen of the Helper Dogs center. She gruffly tolerated the tiny puppies and could bring herself every now and then to approve of some of the male dogs, but she hated the females. If she thought they needed reminding of this, or bringing into line for any number of things, she told them so in no uncertain terms.

Queenie would usually be tied up to the wall by the time we arrived, and all the Helper Dogs trainees would join her, tethered to posts around the hall with a chew or a toy to distract them while the puppy parents drew chairs into a circle and discussed progress in the center of the room. Learning how to wait patiently was an important part of the training, as, in their professional roles, the dogs would often be called upon to sit quietly for hours, perhaps under the desk at their partner's office. The more obedient they were, the more likely they'd be tolerated and even welcomed in all the public situations where their help was really needed. Keeping the puppies tied up in the room also helped with their advanced training: at Helper Dogs HQ, they'd have to sit and wait their turn before being put through their paces individually by their trainer, and it appreciably shortened their training time if they watched the other dogs performing the tasks expected of them first.

But of course, as a learning experience, it was very hard for the bouncy small puppies. They didn't know the reason they were being tethered to the wall, and they often let their puppy parent and everyone else know they didn't think much of this treatment by whining or barking loudly. To remedy the bad behavior it was usually sufficient to praise them when they were quiet and to ignore their outbursts—standard Helper Dogs procedure—but sometimes something more was required, and Jamie would take the dreaded bark collar out of the cupboard when he could stand the noise no longer. This was something he'd borrowed from the obedience classes, and it didn't hurt the dogs; however, whenever the dog barked, a small box on the collar let off a citrus smell, an odor that was a hundred times more pungent to their sensitive noses than to ours. Dogs didn't like it, and I hated it.

Once, when Emma was young and Jo wasn't around to look after her during my hospital visit, I dropped her off at the center instead. Yvonne, a new puppy parent, took the leash from me when I got there and led her into an obedience class. Jamie promised to look after her for the rest of the morning's classes if I was delayed. All morning, as my waiting time stretched out ahead of me, and each appointment got moved back, I didn't fret because I knew she was in good hands. I just took a deep breath and thought about my Emma to take my mind off the unpleasant tests I was waiting to undergo.

When I returned to the training center, I was horrified to see her lying cramped in a crate built for the very youngest of puppies, looking very sorry for herself and wearing the bark collar.

"I'm sorry," apologized Jamie. "She just wouldn't be quiet and she was disrupting all the other classes. I had to do it."

I felt physically sick as I took the seemingly huge collar off her little neck.

"I'm so sorry," I whispered into her fur. I'd never have left her if I'd thought for one second it wasn't going to be a pleasurable experience for her.

From then on even the sight of the bark collar made her unhappy. Some puppies, on the other hand, never experienced the bark collar. They were either too clever, too obedient or simply too dopey. It was completely alien to Elvis, who didn't mind sitting on his blanket and being tethered, and never barked to show his displeasure once during the whole time I knew him. He'd just chew his chew and then lie down and fall fast asleep.

Another lesson Emma had to learn the hard way was to respect her elders and betters. For some reason she didn't register that Queenie's growls and snarls meant it was a good idea to keep away from her. Uncharacteristically, we'd arrived early at the class one day, and I was chatting away to Jamie while we waited for the other dogs to arrive. Emma was now five months old and was well behaved enough to wander around without a lead on—or so I thought. From behind my back I suddenly heard a large, gruff bark, and a menacing rumble from the back of Queenie's throat. My head snapped round and I saw Emma right in front of Queenie, much too close for my liking and definitely too close for Queenie's. She was telling the pup as clearly as possible to clear out of her personal space, but Emma wasn't listening. Another growl came, more forcefully, but Emma just rolled on her back to show her tummy, as if to say: "I'm just a little puppy girl, please don't hurt me"—but not, as Jamie explained to me later, in the proper submissive way she should have been. Queenie was getting really cross. She was just about to lunge when Jamie and I interposed, grabbing Emma and pushing Queenie back. In my arms, Emma wagged her tail and licked my face, oblivious to the danger she'd been in, whereas my heart was pounding and I was trembling.

In the class after the Queenie incident we practiced for a Helper Dogs demonstration day, which had been organized for the following week to show the dogs off to the people who lived near the center. Each dog was demonstrating a different Helper Dog skill that they could perform for their owners. One dog was to pick up and bring the post, another to find and bring slippers; Emma's task was to locate and bring back a mobile phone; Eddie was going to remove a hat and scarf from someone sitting in a wheelchair, and poor old Elvis was supposed to be carefully pulling off his puppy parent's shoes and socks.

Some trainers from the head office came to watch us practice. They seemed pleased with the way the dogs' training was progressing. They watched carefully, taking notes for the duration, and gave a little talk at the end in which they said how impressed they were by the standards at the new center. Then, the Helper Dogs head trainer reeled off a list of dogs who were almost ready to move on. I listened in horror as Emma's name came up, right near the top of the list. The sound of it hung heavy in the still air of the room, and I couldn't quite believe it had actually been said. Emma and Eddie had progressed so fast and so well that they were a credit to the Guide Dog Association that had provided them.

It felt as if someone, somewhere, had made a mistake and three and a half months of my life, the happiest I'd ever had, were about to be taken away from me.

"What about Elvis?" asked Jo. Elvis, though from a different litter, was in the same intake and was therefore about the same age as Eddie and Emma. He was asleep in a pile in the corner of the room, snoring and blissfully unaware that he was being spoken about.

"Needs a bit more time" was the reply.

I wished that Emma needed more time. I wished that she needed lots and lots of time. Forever would be perfect.

Elvis, in fact, never did end up being a Helper Dog. Around forty percent of the dogs that begin their training don't complete it, for a variety of reasons. With some, like a dog I'd met called Sophie, it becomes clear early on that they're not naturally suited to being a successful Helper Dog. Sophie was a very assertive pup who, while very good at home with her puppy parent in a one-to-one situation, found it very hard to concentrate in the much noisier and exciting environment of the puppy classroom. She barked continuously when tethered and would bite through her lead and be off racing around the room if ignored for any length of time. Helper Dogs made every attempt to turn this around, but it wasn't to be, and her parent was allowed to keep her forever as a pet.

Others were too attached to their puppy parent to be successfully placed. Dylan, Emma's playmate whose wobbly long legs and dark coat made him look like Bambi, fell totally and hopelessly in love with his puppy parent, Julia. He'd gaze longingly at her and follow her everywhere around the house and once, when he was still a small puppy, he'd placed himself between her and a noisy abusive drunk when they'd been out for a late evening walk. He was devoted and would have laid down and died for her if she'd asked him. So devoted that Jamie became concerned; a Helper Dog must be able to work with a variety of people, and Dylan only had eyes for Julia. He'd get anxious if he couldn't keep her in sight, and begin whining and crying if she was away too long.

Jamie organized afternoons and classes where Dylan would be alone, in an attempt to lessen the bond, but Dylan couldn't do it, and classes became impossible for him. Then Jamie placed him temporarily with another puppy parent, but all Dylan wanted to do was be with Julia. It was very hard for Julia too. She already suffered from depression and had recently been diagnosed with cancer, and was increasingly relying on Dylan for companionship and support. I felt that Dylan sensed all of this and was upping the love he was giving in response.

It was a difficult time for them both and it put Helper Dogs in a tricky position. On the one hand, I could see that Jamie and Frank both liked Julia and felt for her, and wanted to do all they could to help—in the same way that they were sensitive to my hospital visits and did their best to help me with Emma when I needed it. Yet, on the other hand, Dylan was an expensive asset for them, a good-natured, intelligent puppy that had so much potential to enrich a disabled person's life, and their first duty was to the charity and the people waiting for dogs. I could see that every time the pair came to the center the situation was only going to get more complicated. I raised the subject with Jamie, but he just gave me an agonized look and shrugged his shoulders as if to say, "Your guess is as good as mine." Eventually, it was decided to send Dylan off to an experienced trainer with six dogs of her own who lived far out in the countryside.

I didn't see Dylan leave and could only imagine how utterly heartbreaking it must have been for Julia. For Dylan it went from bad to worse. All of a sudden he was one of seven dogs, and so was receiving much less attention than Julia had lavished upon him and less forbearance than Jamie and Frank had shown. So Dylan went on strike. He refused to take any part in the advanced training classes and stopped eating properly. He was given time off class to adjust, only he didn't. He ran away more than once and then cut his leg badly trying to jump out of an upstairs window. That was the final straw, and the powers that be convened a meeting. Julia, who was by that point in remission, asked if she could take him back as her pet. Helper Dogs agreed and asked her to train him as a demonstration dog.

Demonstration dogs are a crucial asset to the charity, the public face that spreads the word about the charity's good work. A fully trained Helper Dog may occasionally give a demonstration with its disabled partner, but the bulk of the publicity work is done by demonstration dogs who live with able-bodied people, who take them to fêtes, schools, clubs and old-people's homes—anywhere they're invited to—to raise awareness and much-needed cash.

So Dylan got to go home with Julia, where he belonged.

As for Elvis, it was clear to Jo, Jamie and Frank that he

was heading for an F in his exams, so Jo agreed that he be placed with a handler who'd won obedience competitions at Crufts for some intensive training. The problem—and Jo must have known it deep down—was that obedience wasn't the issue. Elvis was perfectly obedient; he simply wasn't very bright and never really a hundred percent sure what it was he was supposed to be doing.

He was so amiable and hardworking that Helper Dogs thought he might be able to be a hearing dog, and Hearing Dogs for the Deaf did give him a fair try, before regretfully declining him because he was just too big and boisterous. Then Elvis tried out for the police, but wasn't right for them, either. He was far too friendly for some police jobs but was very tenacious when asked to find things. Maybe he could be a bomb dog? After a short trial the bomb unit sent him back. Elvis was good at seeking out and locating suspicious packages, but he was also far too good at picking them up and bringing them back to his handlers: bomb dogs are supposed to sit by the "bomb," and are at all costs not meant to touch it, so this was not exemplary bomb dog behavior.

Finally Elvis was placed as a pet with an experienced dog-owning family with a little girl with cerebral palsy, where he soon made himself at home.

Another dog I knew, Angus, was returned by the advanced training center to his puppy parent to become a pet. He didn't make the grade for two reasons—the first being a flaky skin condition, which might have made life difficult for his potential partner and led to unmanageable vet's bills. Secondly, he was very much a farm dog. When in town, some days he would bark at children, some days at men with hats or women with brollies—but you could never tell which one it would be. He was also excellent at chasing and bringing back baby birds, rabbits and once even a pheasant. Like a good retriever should, he brought them all back alive in his soft jaws, but such "treasures," while being OK on country walks, would be awkward or embarrassing with a disabled partner in town. His puppy parent was more than delighted to have him back.

Elvis's future seemed clear, even at the demonstration day, when he first inadvertently bit his parent's toes trying to remove her sock and then ran off with one of her shoes. Emma found the mobile phone quickly and placed it perfectly in my hand. She knew she'd performed well and was obviously feeling very proud of herself.

"What a good girl you are," I said, crouching down to stroke her. It was too hard to think she might be leaving us soon.

As we exited the circle of onlookers, a lady came up to me.

"Excuse me," she said, "my little boy's got cerebral palsy and he sometimes has fits. Would I be able to apply for a Helper Dog to help him?"

I looked around for Jamie, but he was demonstrating the "speak" command with Eddie, who immediately barked when asked. Helper Dogs were normally discouraged from barking, but in certain situations it might be important that they attract attention for their partners.

"Jamie, the boss, is busy," I said. "Come and see Cass instead."

I introduced the woman, whose name was Gina, to Cass, who also had cerebral palsy.

"Blue has made the world of difference to me," she said, indicating her chocolate-brown Lab sitting patiently beside her chair. "It's not just all the useful things he can do, but he's really helped me physically. A year ago I could hardly open my left hand, but because I've been grooming and petting him it's become much stronger and more mobile. Look." Cass showed Gina how she could spread her fingers.

I could see Gina was impressed. "But will they let him have a dog if he has fits?"

"Yes," Cass and I said at once, and then started laughing.

"That'd be no problem at all," Cass said. "The dogs can be trained to put someone in the recovery position if need be, pull a blanket from the back of a wheelchair and bark to call for help. Some dogs can even sense when a fit's imminent."

Later I saw Gina speaking to Jamie. She gave me a thumbs-up sign as she left.

As the day drew to an end, I went to chat with the representatives from HQ, who had brought news of the next batch of Helper Dogs, a litter of tiny four-week-old puppies, which had been seen and assessed. A few had been selected to become Helper Dog trainees at eight weeks, once they'd been weaned and were old enough to leave their mum.

"These will be the Fs," the trainers were saying, showing photographs to us all. I couldn't resist having a look.

"There's a little boy that's just right for you, Meg," Jamie said.

But I didn't answer him. I didn't want to think about having another puppy. I only wanted Emma.

Helper Dogs' policy, where they could, was to take the outgoing puppy and replace it with a new puppy on the same day. Helper Dogs also tried to give the puppy parents a different-sex puppy each time, so there wouldn't be too many comparisons with the one before. Sometimes puppy parents were asked to take the puppy they'd had to HQ, where they were given a new puppy to take back home with them. Other times, their new charge was dropped off at their house. Either way, I didn't like it. The whole switcheroo business, in fact, sounded horrendous. I knew we were expected to take a new puppy when Emma left us, but I didn't want Emma to go, so I blocked out all thoughts about it.

Ian came over with two vanilla ice creams, one as a special treat for Emma. It was gone in a few large licks, and as she hopefully turned her attention toward my cone, I looked into her loving, trusting eyes and my vision clouded with tears.

10

Ever since we'd met, Ian and I had been very much a twosome. It had been just the two of us visiting comedy clubs before we were married, the two of us on Waikiki Beach saying our vows and just the two of us on our weekend walks and our visits to comedy clubs as man and wife, although now our family circle had widened to include Emma. I'd introduced Ian to all my old friends, but because we were so wrapped up in our new married life—and now all head over heels about Emma—somehow my connection to them had weakened and we didn't seem to have as much in common as we used to. Gradually, new friends took their place, mostly sharing our newfound passion for dogs.

Coming from a previously dog-free zone, it really surprised me how many dog-lovers there were and how much more everyone seemed to know about dogs than me. They were always full of useful advice on how to get your dog to behave or how to clean and groom it, and Florence even gave me my first dog recipe book. When Emma was sick one day, I was advised to give her plenty of water but no solids, and then give her some homemade chicken and rice in the evening. Emma loved it, and whenever she had an upset tummy, the chicken and rice seemed to fix it. Subsequently, I tried making homemade dog treats and they went down a storm, not just with Emma but with just about every other dog we met.

"Got any new dog treats?" Jamie would ask.

I was by far the least experienced dog owner, and quite often made the most basic of mistakes, but I was fast becoming the most experienced canine chef.

"Some of those look so good I'm tempted to try them myself," Sadie said one day at Helper Dogs. It was the first time Sadie had been back to Helper Dogs since she'd given up Cherry, the black Lab puppy she'd been looking after. Sadie wasn't going to be a puppy parent again as she'd found it too traumatic giving Cherry up.

Because I was busy with my new life, I hadn't had time to wonder how my old friends were getting on, when out of the blue I had a phone call.

"Meg, it's Gemma."

"Gemma!" I squawked, as you do when taken by surprise by a familiar voice on the end of the phone.

We'd known each other since we were students and had lived in the same halls of residence and then the same shared house. Gemma had had an abortion just before she started university and had found it very hard to come to terms with it. We used to sit up talking all night and we became very close.

"Sometimes I dream I can hear a baby crying and I know it's my baby," she'd say. "They say it's just cells, don't they? It couldn't feel anything, but I can still hear it. I wake up thinking it's in the room with me. But there's nothing there."

The abortion had changed Gemma's thoughts about motherhood.

"I never want to have a baby," she said. "It'd just remind me of what happened."

When she was in her early thirties, she'd married and

moved to Devon, and we weren't as in touch as we'd once been.

We exchanged pleasantries and news for a few minutes while I wondered what had occasioned the unexpected call.

"You're never going to believe it . . ." said Gemma finally.

I had a sinking feeling that I might.

"I'm pregnant."

Before I could say anything a torrent of glad tidings poured out of her.

"I know, can you believe it, me of all people? The one who said she never ever wanted children. I didn't even know if I would be able to have them because I'd left it so late. I didn't tell you before because, you know, they say it's bad luck before it's definite. Need to be three months gone at least."

"So how pregnant are you?" I asked. I was trying to keep my tone light, as if I were asking about the weather. I felt slightly spaced out. In the room and on the phone, but not in the room and not on the phone at the same time.

"Seven months—it could be born at any time! It's so exciting and a bit scary. Alan is over the moon. Well, you know he always wanted children even though I didn't."

Ian spoke into the speakerphone.

"That's great news, Gemma," he said.

"Yes, congratulations," I said.

"Thanks. You'll have to come and visit when the baby's born."

"Yes, yes, of course! It'd be lovely to see you." My voice was bright and shiny but brittle, and I felt it could snap and break into a thousand pieces at any time. Some part of me, the part that had known and loved Gemma and Alan for years, was so, so pleased for her, but another part of me, the part that was living in the here and now, and was stuck in cycles of Clomid that were seemingly doing more harm than good, was devastated at the news. The first part of me wanted to go and visit them straightaway, but the second part didn't know if I'd be able. I simply wished it could have been as easy for us.

I said goodbye and put the phone down.

Ian hugged me to him and Emma brought Spiky over. I smiled and played tug with her.

"I'll make the dinner," Ian said.

I carried on playing with Emma.

The phone rang again. It was Jamie. "They're thinking of taking Emma and her brother into advanced training in three weeks," he said. "But there'll be another puppy ready for you. That is OK, isn't it?"

There was a long silence as I let the news sink in. Three weeks. No time at all.

I put the phone down once again, feeling like maybe I should throw the handset—if not the source, then definitely the conduit, of so much troubling news in so short a space of time—through the window and into the garden.

Ian was looking at me.

"I don't know how I'm going to bear letting her go," I said. "I feel like my heart is being ripped out."

And how was Emma supposed to understand why she was being sent away?

"She'll think she's done something wrong and that we don't want her any more," I said as the tears started streaming down my face. "That she wasn't good enough." Once I'd started crying I couldn't stop. Huge sobs at the thought of our little puppy girl not understanding why she couldn't stay with us, the people who loved her.

"She tries so hard to be good and do everything we ask of her. How is she supposed to know that if we could keep her we would? We'd do anything to keep her but we . . ."

I dissolved into sobs, for Emma, for Gemma, for Ian and for me.

"We could try to buy her off them," said Ian, "if you're really definitely sure you want to."

"Of course I want to. Don't you want to keep her too?"

"I do. She's our little girl."

Then I remembered why we had her. "W-what about the disabled person who needs her? What about them?"

"We could give them enough money so they could buy two puppies or even three or four."

"They couldn't refuse, could they?"

"Charities always need money."

"They couldn't refuse ten thousand pounds."

"Ten thousand pounds?" Ian said.

"Yes, the money Mum and Dad gave us that we were going to use for the IVF—we'll use that."

Ian looked concerned. "Are you sure? That money . . ."

"Yes, yes, yes, I'm sure. How many new puppies will ten thousand pounds buy?"

"Each puppy is roughly five hundred pounds, so maybe twenty."

Twenty new puppies in exchange for one Emma. That seemed a good deal to me. She was worth more than twenty puppies to me, but she couldn't be worth more than that to them.

"I don't see how they could resist," Ian said. "But I don't want you to regret—"

"I won't regret it!" I shouted. "How could I when it means we'll get to keep Emma?"

Emma had by now fallen asleep on the sofa.

"And Helper Dogs will be OK," I said. "They'll have twenty new puppies. And Emma hasn't even gone for her advanced training yet. She might not even be suitable as a Helper Dog. Even if we gave her up she might not make it."

We both knew that that was a lie. Emma would make a great Helper Dog for someone, but I couldn't, I just couldn't, bear the thought of letting her go.

"The IVF clinic . . ." Ian started to say. But I didn't want to talk about that.

"Shall we phone Jamie?"

"I think it'd be better if we put our request in writing," Ian said. "Then they have to take it seriously. Put it before the board."

We drafted the letter that night. If we were allowed to keep Emma, it'd probably mean I couldn't continue to be a part of Helper Dogs anymore. Unless perhaps they'd want her to be a demonstration dog. Emma would be a great demonstration dog; she loved children and was so friendly. Maybe, I hoped, a combination of the money and offering her services as a demonstration dog would be enough for them to let us keep her.

I told Jamie what we were planning to do.

"I think you should take a trip down to the Helper Dogs Head Office," he said, his voice heavy and serious. "Take the letter to them in person."

So we did. Emma was very good on the long journey in the back of the car. Traffic was horrendous and it took more than four hours to get there, deep into Hertfordshire where somebody had left the charity a beautiful Tudor mansion and its grounds in their will. The main house held the charity's offices, and its great hall was used for doggy graduation ceremonies. Then there were stables and other more modern buildings dotted across the acres: accommodation for disabled people who came to meet potential partner dogs and attend courses, the dog kennels, and the dog training and exercise areas. It was very impressive and looked like it would be a lovely place to work.

I bristled when I saw Diane, the puppy parent from Peterborough. I'd hoped I'd never have to see her again.

Emma, however, was delighted to see her.

"Has she tried this?" Diane asked, pulling a tube of Primula cheese and ham from her waist bag. "It's a very good way of teaching dogs the correct position they should be in when they're walking at your side."

She opened the tube and squirted a little bit out so Emma could have a taste. Emma thought it was very fine indeed and wanted some more. Diane held the cheese down at her side and Emma trotted along beside her in the perfect position.

"You should always have the lead relaxed in your hand because the dogs can pick up if you're tense," she said.

I was actually feeling very tense. Ian had gone upstairs to the offices to find Henry, who was in charge, to give him the letter.

Diane was stroking Emma's lead. "Just smoothing out the lead like this can calm a distressed dog down," she said.

Emma rolled over onto her tummy. "And here," Diane said, "where her hips join her tummy—that crease, that can be very soothing too." I looked down at Emma. She certainly seemed to be enjoying it.

"Thank you," I said.

Henry came back down with Ian and took us on a tour of the site. We visited the kennels where most of the dogs stayed while completing advanced training, and Ian and I exchanged a smile, perhaps the first time I had smiled all weekend. We were pleased to see that each kennel, which was the size of a small room and held one or two dogs, also had a little sofa for the dogs to sit on. We'd got into trouble when Emma was little for letting her sit on the sofa (it wasn't recommended, for fear that she'd get ideas above her station), but now we felt that if Helper Dogs provided their dogs with sofas then we were only helping with her training. We then went through into the "shop," where the dogs were taught how to take food—boxes of cornflakes, tins of baked beans, packets of rice or pasta—off the shelves when asked. People in wheelchairs can have difficulty taking items from the lower and higher shelves in supermarkets, and often the dogs become so good at their job that they automatically drop their owner's favorite food into their baskets. I smiled again as I imagined Emma sneakily putting her favorite treats into the basket while her partner wasn't looking. Then I caught myself. If we were successful, she wouldn't be going anywhere.

Finally Henry opened the door to a small meeting room with ten or so people and two dogs in it.

"They couldn't make the main graduation ceremony so

we've organized a small one just for them," he explained.

At the front of the room a man on crutches with his black Helper Dog Labrador sitting beside him was speaking eloquently about all his dog, Zorba, had done for him.

"I'd never been much of a doggy person before I got Zorba. Too hairy and dribbly and much too inclined to lick their bottoms for my liking," he said, and everyone laughed. "Huh! Little did I know. Since I became disabled Zorba has become everything to me. He goes with me to work every morning. Hands over my wallet to pay for my lunch in the cafeteria—they usually have something tasty for him too—goes out with me in the evenings and falls asleep with me at night, on my bed no less. His hairy, slobbery face is the first thing I see each morning and I wouldn't have it any other way.

"Seriously, though," he continued, "the truth is I probably wouldn't be around still if it wasn't for him. I used to suffer from depression before I became disabled and I suffered from it a lot more afterward. 'Why me?' I used to ask. 'What did this have to happen to me for?'"

He shook his head as he remembered. "I had some very dark times, times when I didn't see the point of going on. When the pills by my bed seemed like the only alternative.

"It was my psychiatrist who suggested I got a dog. I thought it was a crazy idea and told him he needed counseling himself, but he was right. Having Zorba took me out of myself. I couldn't mope around when Zorba needed taking out, and once we were out, people were always wanting to come over and talk to us. Zorba made it impossible for me to keep being miserable all the time.

"I went back to work—I'm a lecturer in screenwriting.

Zorba comes to work with me every day and keeps me and the students in line. Although I do find my students are writing an awful lot of scripts about dogs these days—especially ones about black Labradors!"

At the end of his speech, everyone clapped.

Then Steph wheeled herself to the front, her Golden Retriever, Bridie, close beside her. As soon as she started to speak it was easy to tell that she was very nervous. She read from a piece of paper, and both it and her voice shook as she spoke.

"I don't know what to say, I'm not used to speaking in front of people, nothing is enough to tell you how grateful I am." She looked at her Helper Dog and a tear ran down her face. Then, unable to speak, she handed the piece of paper to the master of ceremonies to read out:

"As soon as I met Bridie, I fell in love with her and wanted her to be my Helper Dog. All the way through training, I was sure that somebody was going to say she wasn't suitable, as I'd never had a dog before, but Bridie did everything perfectly even when I got some of the commands wrong. The first day she came to live with me I was so happy I felt like I'd won the lottery. But I was wrong about that—having Bridie is much better than winning the lottery."

Steph smiled through her tears. Bridie put her paws on her lap to comfort her.

I looked at Ian. I wanted to cry too. Several people in the room were. Yet still I didn't want to let Emma go.

We thanked Henry, whom I felt had been very gracious with us given that we were coming in and disrupting all his plans. I was on tenterhooks. I hadn't dared ask Ian while we were still in the faded, grand old house what had gone on upstairs. As we walked back to the car with Emma, who was panting happily, I gave him a meaningful look.

"They'll let us know after they've had a meeting to discuss it," he said.

11

Ian was at work when the envelope with the Helper Dogs logo on it finally arrived.

I phoned to tell him it was there.

"Open it," he said.

But I couldn't. I was too scared. Too much rested on this letter. I took Emma for a long walk by the river but got nothing else done all day as I waited for Ian to come home.

At last he arrived, and I removed myself to the lounge to let him open it in the kitchen. It seemed to be taking him an awfully long time.

"Have you opened it yet?" I called out anxiously.

"They've said no."

I sank down on the sofa, feeling sick. Emma jumped up next to me and I stroked her soft fur.

"Our mission statement is that each one of our dogs should reach its highest potential and so far Emma has given every indication that she will make an excellent Helper Dog one day . . ." said Ian, but I couldn't concentrate on what he was saying. All I kept thinking, over and over again, was that they'd said no. It was too awful to even cry about.

"She will make a good Helper Dog," Ian said.

Even if I'd wanted to agree—and I knew he was right— I couldn't speak to reply.

*

Ian made our dinner and I gave Emma hers. I felt numb, hardly even managing to smile when Emma did her latest trick of picking up her bowl and bringing it over to me to put a treat in at the end of her meal.

"They'll be nice to her, won't they, whoever she's partnered with?" I asked Ian. "They'll love her too. They'll love her like we do, and be gentle and kind."

"No one could love her like we do," Ian whispered.

We decided to take Emma to all of her favorite places for one last visit before she left us. First, that weekend, was the County Park where she'd first swam and so many times enjoyed playing with Eddie and Elvis and all her other friends. There was a long strip of sand there on which, ever since we'd been to the seaside, she'd taken to racing, up and down, up and down, up and down, with delight, bottom tucked under, a crazy run of happy abandonment. This time, though, I couldn't bear to watch.

The next day, I took her to the local park to meet up with Sadie and her pet dog, Misha. Sadie was still trying to get over giving up her Helper Dog puppy a few months before. Her dog, Cherry, had always been borderline, and she'd been hoping that she'd be returned to her. Cherry had injured her hips when she was a young puppy and had not been allowed to run free for almost six months and had undergone hydrotherapy. She'd recovered enough that it had been decided to take her in for advanced training. The news so far was that although they were doing everything they could, she might not be a Helper Dog. None of her brothers and sisters had made the grade, but they weren't giving up on Cherry yet.

"I know she'd be happier with me," Sadie said.

I nodded my agreement. Maybe all puppy parents felt like this, maybe they all just fell helplessly in love. To get the best from the puppies you have to put everything into it—affection, time, blood, sweat and tears. It has to be that way for them to flourish and grow up to be the best Helper Dog possible: they must trust you completely and want to do anything for you. But the inevitable consequence is a broken heart when it's time to say goodbye.

I didn't want to let Emma go, but I'd reluctantly come around to accepting that I was going to have to. In the meantime we kept going on our favorite walks and playing our favorite games, and every now and again I'd have a cry at the hopelessness of it all. I tried not to: in those last few weeks I wanted to give her a lifetime's worth of love and happiness, and the best memories of country parks

and interesting smells and doggy friends to play with—just in case there wasn't much of that in store for her in her future life.

All the while, I'd been going through my fertility routines in a sort of daze. Vitamins all the time, a healthy diet and constant efforts to resist that second glass of wine. Every day, as soon as I woke, before standing up even, I'd get the thermometer out and take my temperature. Clomid on days three to seven of my cycle; then, on days twelve to sixteen of my cycle, ovulation sticks to test if and when I was ovulating. As soon as the test turned pink, Ian needed to be ready for action. Poor man.

I was following the prescriptions dutifully, unthinkingly, since our difficulties with conception had taken a back seat to the present crisis with our puppy girl; in fact, I reflected, when it came to the crucial moment, I'd offered without a moment's hesitation to give up our IVF money for the chance to keep Emma.

I awoke from my daze one morning to a startling fact. There was no hiding it: I was two weeks late. Even by my erratic cycles this was too much to ignore, but it was impossible, I said to myself. I couldn't be. I didn't dare hope that in the midst of this dark period I might finally be pregnant. I bought a pregnancy test, but the line didn't turn red. Maybe it was faulty. I bought another one, and then another.

The pregnancy tests weren't showing that I was pregnant, but on the Internet forums there were lots of women who'd had negative pregnancy tests yet had been pregnant anyway. I also remembered what Carmel had said about the line on her test being so faint that she could barely see it. The doctors had thought she was mad, but she'd been pregnant. Another day passed and no change, and I began to convince myself I really might be. I so wanted to be. I even told a couple of old friends that I met up with at a convention that I thought I was, just to see how it felt for the words to roll off my tongue, pass my lips and take flight into the world.

"Still very early days yet," I said, as I accepted their congratulations. I was sure there was a little person growing inside me. The little person we'd been waiting so long for.

"You'll make a lovely mum," one of them said.

On Monday I decided I'd go to the doctor. The pregnancy tests were still showing negative, but maybe they just weren't sensitive enough; doctors, the forums also said, had more sensitive tests at their disposal, and it would let me know for certain, be sure about the life that was growing inside me. I phoned for an appointment but my regular doctor wasn't there. Did I mind seeing another doctor instead? I could see the other doctor today, within the next hour in fact, whereas I couldn't see my own doctor until the end of the week. I put my jacket on, gave Emma a chew to keep her occupied and got in the car.

When I got to the surgery, I was informed by the receptionist that the new doctor was videoing all his patients as part of his final training. I said I didn't mind being filmed, took a seat and flicked through a tatty magazine in a bid to block out of my range of vision the posters on the wall giving dietary advice to expectant mums. Then I got to thinking that actually I did mind, and went back to the receptionist and told her that I'd rather not be videoed.

"That's OK," she said. "It's just for him to see his bedside manner, that sort of thing. It's perfectly within your rights. I'll ask him not to."

I went into the treatment room. The video camera was placed facing the doctor and the patient's chair next to him.

"I don't want to be videoed," I said.

"It's not on," he said, a young man with short light hair and a small mustache, smartly dressed in dark trousers and a stripy shirt.

There was an orange light flashing on the camera, but I presumed that meant it was on standby. I looked at him.

"Why's the light flashing?"

He turned the camera so it was facing away from us.

"Now what can I do for you?"

He was a little difficult to understand. When he'd come into the waiting room and loudly announced the patient's name before mine, he'd had to say it three times before a man sitting in the opposite corner finally realized it was him being called. I told him that I thought I might be pregnant because I was late. I also told him that I'd taken more than one pregnancy test and they had all come back negative. He must have my notes, I said, so I hoped I didn't have to go into the saga of my hospital visits and my medical history too closely. Was it possible for him to do a more sensitive, accurate test, I asked, then fell silent and looked at him hopefully through watering eyes.

He looked through the notes, shuffled through them, and then read them a second time before speaking. I strained to make sense of his words.

"It is highly, highly unlikely that you are pregnant," he said. "In fact, given your age and prognosis so far, it is doubtful, almost impossible, in fact, that you will ever be pregnant."

I stumbled out of the treatment room wishing that he had filmed our brief, painful chat, so he could watch it later and feel ashamed—and then hopefully improve on how he talked to patients.

I had been unsure whether to tell Ian about my visit to the doctor, but a whirlwind of events that afternoon overtook my indecision and saw to it that he never knew.

My brother Jack phoned: "Carmel's had the baby."

"Oh! Oh, good. Is she OK? What did she have?" My heart was filling with joy for them, but, with the day I'd had, it was having difficulty transmitting itself through my brain and into my voice. I struggled to rouse myself.

"A little girl. We're going to call her Maisie," said Jack.

"Maisie's a lovely—"

"She's in the premature baby unit," Jack interrupted. "The birth was awful. She shouldn't have been born yet, but they said they had to take her out of Carmel or she might have died. At one time I thought both the baby and Carmel were going to die. She wouldn't stop bleeding."

His voice cracked.

"They . . . they don't know if the baby's going to have brain damage. She didn't breathe for a long, long time. But she's alive and I didn't think she was going to be . . . Can you come?"

I dropped Emma at Jo's and caught the train to London, got on another train into Kent, then caught a taxi to the hospital. Carmel had been given a room of her own and was being closely monitored.

"How are you?"

She smiled weakly. "Sore and swollen. The midwife said I was bleeding too much, so I had to have a blood transfusion," she said, prostrate on her pillows. "It happens more often with black women—we're more at risk—but we've got a baby . . ." A tear slipped down her face. "She's so beautiful. Go and see her."

Jack took me to the premature baby unit. There were six see-through incubators with round hand holes in one side. In one corner another mother sat gazing into the incubator at her baby.

"Here's Maisie," Jack said, stopping beside a cot. Inside was a tiny, tiny shriveled little girl with a shock of black hair. "You can touch her."

We washed our hands with the sanitizer and I put my hand through the hole. I stroked her miniature leg gently and she moved a touch.

"The nurse said it has to be a more definite stroke," Jack said. "Don't know why, but she said they get irritated by flickery strokes; maybe it's like being tickled."

I tried a firmer stroke and Maisie opened her eyes and seemed to look at me.

"Hello, Maisie. Welcome to the world."

I sat with Jack and Carmel for the afternoon until it was time for me to go back to London and meet Ian to get the train home.

"So, how have you been?" Jack asked as I was gathering my bags together.

"Oh, fine. Fine. You know, just the usual sort of stuff." I hugged him. "She's lovely—whether she has brain damage or whether she's fine, which I think she will be, Maisie's a lovely, lovely little girl."

12

The night before Emma was to leave us we hardly slept. She lay on our bed, unsure of where this privilege had come from, or why, and I stroked her as I lay awake.

Ian was up at dawn to go to work as usual, but not before he served up the last puppy breakfast, complete with a final rendition of his "Puppy Breakfast-time" song. He also managed a quick play in the paddling pool with her, carefully shielding his suit from any splashes as he threw her ball and plastic duck into the water for her to retrieve. She loved the paddling pool and had even been introducing her friends to it, such as Eddie, who'd jumped straight in when he'd come around to play. Liz had been amazed; Eddie didn't usually even like getting his feet wet and would hold each paw up for Liz to dry when he came in from the muddy garden or a rainy walk. As we stood there, watching the dogs play, we reminisced about the times they'd shared and how we'd watched them grow up together. We were both upset and apprehensive about letting our puppies go, and took comfort in talking about all the good times we'd had.

One recollection sparked another and another, and I thought that we shouldn't have been surprised at anything the two of them did. Once, when they were both young puppies, they'd managed to tip a tin of white paint over in the garden and then had made rows of little white paw prints across the patio before we could stop them. Fortunately, Ian had been able to get the white paint off with a high-pressure hose. "I'm going to miss her so much," I said.

"If only we could have kept them for a year," said Liz, "like some other charities do."

"I don't know how I'm going to love the new puppy."

"Me neither," Liz agreed. "I feel like I need a break before the next one arrives."

But Helper Dogs was always short of volunteers and needed to keep the ones it had occupied. I could see how a small break might easily turn into a longer one, but it didn't make it any easier for me. Loving a puppy and then losing it, a conveyor belt of lost love. I just wasn't sure.

After Ian had left for work, I toured the house looking at all of Emma's things while she lazed on the patio in the June sun. Bowls, brushes, blankets, a basket; leads, food, towels, treats and more than a hundred toys. There was so much—physical evidence of the giant space she'd come to occupy in our hearts and lives. I couldn't imagine what we'd done before she'd been here, and I didn't want to think about how our little house would seem when she'd gone. Soon, I was just wandering around empty rooms in order to avoid looking at the pile of stuff in the hall. There was nothing I could do to delay any longer. I packed the boot, Emma jumped into the car, onto her pink princess car seat, and I drove us the fifteen minutes or so to the Helper Dogs center.

I was determined not to cry on the way. I didn't want to cause an accident, and my crying might have been distressing and confusing for my pup, which didn't seem fair. I had almost cried in the car once before, after a hospital appointment, but somehow I'd managed not to until I'd pulled up in the Helper Dogs car park. Jamie had innocently asked how I was and then I couldn't stop. Loud, nose-sniffing sobs: Emma had been very worried.

"It's all right, it's all right," I tried to soothe her, but as we walked down the quiet country lane adjacent to the Helper Dogs center she wouldn't take her eyes off me. Emma knew something was up. No matter what happened, though, I wasn't going to cry, not until she was gone. I wanted Emma to remember me as happy and smiling—the way I usually was. I didn't want her to think even for one millisecond that I was leaving her with Jamie because she'd done something wrong.

"I'd better go," I said, when I'd unloaded all of Emma's toys.

"I bet Head Office has never met a dog who has this many toys before!" Jamie said.

I stroked Emma. "She'll be OK, won't she?"

"Yes, you know she will. And we'll get reports on how she's getting on every now and again. We'll keep you in touch with her."

I hesitated, unwilling to say anything or move a muscle.

"It's OK," Jamie said. "Look, it's best if you go quickly—it's easier for you and her. I'll give you a call as soon as I have your new puppy."

I nodded and then turned away and walked to the car,

conscious of every step I was taking away from her, knowing that Emma was watching me all the way. I watched her watching me in the rearview mirror as I started the engine.

I couldn't hear what Jamie was saying, but it looked something like: "Come on, Emma, this way." She went with him and disappeared into the center.

By the time I got back it was almost one o'clock and Ian, who'd only worked a half day, was already home. He opened the door and held me close in his arms as I finally let the tears come. I couldn't let myself cry for long, but for now I couldn't help it. Jamie had another little puppy for us, a new dog to love while the shock of losing Emma was still red raw.

"I don't know how I'm going to love him," I confessed to Ian. "I don't even know if I'm going to be able to like him."

"You will, of course you will," Ian soothed, still holding me tight.

I was sure that I would never ever be able to love this new puppy as much as I'd loved Emma. Deep down, I felt like he was trying to take Emma's place; maybe, if the new puppy hadn't been ready and waiting to come to us—he was nearly eight weeks old—then Emma wouldn't have needed to leave quite so quickly. She could have stayed for a few more weeks. Even a few more days, a single day, and I would have had a little more time with her.

She'd be almost at Head Office by now and would be worried about me, wondering where I was. I wrote the last part of her diary newspaper column:

This morning Meg made me a special breakfast of scrambled eggs and bacon and then she took me for a walk by the river and had a bit of a cry while I played in the long grass. When we got home she packed up all my toys and my bed and my food and my treats.

She gave me lots of strokes and a hug when she said goodbye. She told me I'm a big puppy girl now and ready for the next stage of my training. She said I'll be the best Helper Dog ever, but if there's ever a time when I can't be a Helper Dog I could come back and live with her and Ian and that would make them the happiest people in the world.

I e-mailed the column to the newspaper along with a photo of her wearing her Helper-Dog-in-training coat, staring into the camera with trusting brown eyes.

I sniffed back my tears. Before the new puppy arrived I had yet another hospital appointment.

At the hospital I sat for ages in the Obstetrics waiting room, where every second woman seemed to be very heavily pregnant. When I was finally seen, my doctor announced that she wouldn't be around for my next appointment as she was going on maternity leave. I looked down at her belly area. I didn't know why I'd never noticed before, but she had a distinct bump.

"This is the best I've seen so far," she said, as she scanned me to see if the follicle was growing inside me. "Make the most of it."

She gave me a meaningful look. She didn't know my heart was breaking from losing one puppy and worried about gaining another. Sex was the last thing on my mind.

"You'll be seen once every three months from now on," she said. Despite the good things going on inside me, I didn't think this sounded too promising—maybe they were cutting down on my appointments because there was no point in me coming more often. Time had been against me from the start, and now it seemed as if they were letting it pass without effort.

"But I could . . . I could still get pregnant, couldn't I?" I said.

"Oh, yes," she replied. "All you need is that extra bit of luck."

I sighed. Luck was in such short supply.

As I left the hospital I wondered how Emma was getting on. I hoped she wasn't confused and sad. I hoped the dog trainers at advanced training would be kind to her. Then I started to feel sorry for the new puppy, guilty that I wasn't almost bursting with excitement as I had been at the thought of Emma's arrival. Poor little thing: he was going to be leaving his mum and his brothers and sisters for the first time today. He'd be feeling frightened and confused too. I decided to go to the pet superstore and buy him something nice to play with. We'd almost completely exhausted their selection of toys with Emma—she'd had the ones she liked and spurned the remainder—and the prospect of buying more new treats to make a new puppy happy almost gladdened my heart.

There, in the giant pet store, I found Liz wandering the aisles, eyes red-rimmed from crying. She'd had to give up Eddie today too, and as soon as she saw me, she started to cry again.

We gave each other a big hug and then consoled ourselves over a coffee at the next-door café.

"He was such a good little boy," she said. "It's so hard to let him go."

"How have your children been taking it?" I asked. Liz had three boys aged seven, ten and eleven.

"Not as badly as me," Liz said. "I did lots of explaining when he first came to us about how although he was staying with us for a while he wasn't really ours and would have to go away after a few months. I think it helped that I used to work for a dog-sitting service, so they've seen dogs come and go in the past—although none like Eddie, of course. This morning there were a few tears, but mainly hugs, and then my youngest, Tony, asked me when the next puppy would be arriving even before Eddie was out of the door. Kids!"

She sniffled and smiled at the same time.

"I haven't stopped crying since he left, but I've managed to be 'sensible' Mum in front of the kids. I've got to get myself together for when they get home from school."

I left the pet store with Liz, having bought my new puppy a soft furry blanket to sit on, a snake toy (because it had been one of Emma's favorites) and a very soft blue-and-white stuffed dog.

When I got home, Jamie's van was outside our house. Either he'd brought Emma back, which was highly unlikely, or the new puppy was already here.

13

"Meet Mr. Pup-Pup," said Ian as he opened the front door, plonking something completely unrecognizable into my outstretched arms. A bright almost-white wriggling little furry fluffball, more like a miniature polar bear than a puppy, as different from Emma as could be.

"Hello," I said. "Hello, little puppy."

At eight weeks old he was a lot more boisterous than Emma had been when she first arrived. He twisted and turned from back to front, nibbled at my long hair and then licked my face.

"His Helper Dogs name is Freddy," said Jamie, giving Ian a look.

"Mr. Pup-Pup," Ian mouthed at me and I tried hard not to grin.

Jamie and Ian had been entertaining Mr. Pup-Pup for the past hour.

"Why didn't you call me and let me know he was here?" I asked.

"Because we thought you'd be back at any minute."

"I went to buy him some toys from the pet shop and I met Liz there."

"How was she?" Jamie asked.

"Tearful."

I might have been tearful too, but it was hard to laugh and cry at the same time, and Freddy, wriggling in my arms and yapping his tiny puppy-dog yap, was winning the battle.

I put him on the floor and he scampered around and then ran back to me.

"Has he come far?" He didn't seem at all tired from his journey.

"No, Summer Road," Jamie said. That explained his energy. Summer Road was only just over a mile away. "It's the breeder's first litter, and she got in touch to ask if we might be interested in taking one or two of them. There were two boys we thought looked promising for us, but this one was better at retrieving—although neither of them were all that enthusiastic. Little terrors, weren't you?"

Jamie's attention had been drawn back to the furball; it was difficult to keep your eyes off him—he was just too bouncy and cute. Jamie wriggled the toy rattler in front of Freddy, and Freddy pounced on it as if he was a kitten and shook it with delight.

"No good at doing what you were supposed to when I wanted you to," he said to the dog, who was now growling and playing tug-of-war with the subdued snake. "But then that's puppies for you. Anyway, he's yours," said Jamie, standing up decisively, dusting himself down and taking his leave.

I shut the front door as he retreated, while restraining the pup and making a mental note to ask Ian to get the stair guard out of the loft. Then I gave Freddy (or Mr. Pup-Pup, as Ian insisted on calling him) some of the food the breeder had been giving him along with a small amount of Helper Dogs' puppy food. He scoffed it all up, and I took him outside to use the toilet area, but it was all too far and too much for him, and he'd weed on the lawn before he'd reached it.

After that, we went back inside, and fed, watered and tired out, he fell fast asleep on the rug.

"He looks so sweet," I said. "And he seems so confident for such a young puppy."

Half an hour later Freddy was awake, recharged and ready for more fun and games, with the boundless energy that puppies have. Then a quick sleep, then more games, but when it came to bedtime he didn't want to go into his crate, which we'd placed on the floor of our bedroom. He barked, whined and bit at the bars with his tiny teeth and scratched at the floor in distress, and I simply couldn't stand it. With so much heartbreak already in the day, I didn't want to see him sad on his first night with us. He was such a little boy and he'd only just left his family; it was his first night away from home and all he'd previously known.

"He'll calm down," Ian said. "He'll tire himself out and fall asleep."

But ten minutes later Freddy still hadn't calmed down— if anything, he'd got worse.

"I can't bear it," I said. "Let him out of the crate. He can sleep on the floor for tonight."

It was totally against what Helper Dogs advised, but I opened the wire door anyway. Freddy was delighted, his tiny tail wagging wildly.

Ian made him a little bed on the floor.

"That's it, night night, Mr. Pup-Pup. You sleep there."

But Freddy didn't want to sleep on the floor. He started yapping and crying and trying to scramble on the bed. It was almost midnight and Ian rolled over grumpily. He had to be up at five for the long journey to London and work.

I climbed out of bed and carried Freddy downstairs to the garden. Once there he raced around and did a wee, ran back inside and nosed around, then had a long drink of water.

Above us I could hear the sound of Ian sleeping, fortifying himself for another commute and a long day at work. He worked so hard to support us and he really needed his rest. I pulled out an old blanket from the cupboard.

"We'll sleep down here tonight," I told Freddy, who seemed to think this was an excellent plan. I lay down on the sofa and Freddy curled up on the floor with his blue-and-white soft dog toy and fell fast asleep. Staring at the unfamiliar ceiling, with a sofa cushion behind my head and the light angling strangely through the room, I listened to Freddy's little snuffles and snores and hoped Emma was sleeping well wherever she was.

Jamie wasn't pleased when I told him Freddy hadn't slept in the right place.

"You must start as you mean to go on," he said. "Freddy has to get used to sleeping in his crate at night. First of all in the bedroom and then downstairs."

The next day I tried to encourage Freddy to go into his crate by putting tasty treats inside, but he was having none of it. He was small enough for us to easily put him into his crate, whether he wanted to go or not, but it seemed very cruel, and we then had to listen to him whining and crying and barking to be set free.

"You have to do it," Jamie said. "It's part of a Helper Dog's training and the sooner he gets used to it the better it will be all around." He couldn't understand why Freddy should hate his crate so much. For most dogs the crate is a hidey-hole, a private space and a sanctuary—and it has the bonus for the puppy parents that it protects the furniture from gnawing teeth when they were busy or out of the house.

Reluctantly, we put Freddy into his crate that night, and I forced myself, despite the anguish it caused, not to listen to his yelps and whines telling us he didn't want to be there. Over the next few nights, Freddy responded by weeing or pooing, and often both, in his crate, and then lying in it so that in the morning his white fur was a completely different color. Ian became expert at showering the dog, and I at disinfecting the crate, as each morning I came down to find a bedraggled, penitent-looking puppy in desperate need of a clean peeking out from between the bars.

"He'll soon get used to the crate," Ian said, but I wasn't so sure.

Jamie phoned shortly after 7 a.m. on Freddy's second Saturday with us.

"Jo has had a family emergency and needs someone to look after Elvis for the day. I can't do it. I've phoned everyone I can think of, but nobody's around. I wouldn't normally ask, not when you have such a young puppy there, but . . ." He tailed off.

"Of course we can," I said.

He dropped Elvis off twenty minutes later. It wasn't usual practice to put older and younger puppies together because of the physical mismatch, which could tire the younger one out, but as soon as Elvis came bounding through the door Freddy let him know who was in charge. Elvis tried to help himself to one of Freddy's toys, and Freddy yapped at him and chased him into the garden, where Elvis promptly gobbled up a puppy chew Freddy had left. Freddy chased him back into the house yapping all the time. This was his house and he was boss—albeit a quarter-sized version.

After a while I became concerned that Freddy might get exhausted, so I asked Ian to keep an eye on him while the older dog dragged me down to the river for a walk. Freddy wanted to come, but he hadn't had his injections and had to stay home. It was a relief to let Elvis, bigger and stronger than any dog I'd ever walked, off the leash. He gamboled ahead, but never too far, and then came gamboling back to see if I had a treat for him. He'd bounce forward and back, tail wagging for a treat, but then he disappeared: one second he was running ahead, the next he'd tripped over his own paws, performed a sort of somersault and landed in the river.

"Elvis, Elvis, where are you?" I cried.

I raced over to where he'd gone in. Elvis's head was poking out of the water, looking up at me, but he wasn't moving.

"It's OK, it's OK!" I said, although I didn't really know if it was or not. "You'll be all right. Come on, Elvis, up, up, up!"

If he swam along a little way, he'd be able to clamber up the bank. Elvis didn't move.

"This way, Elvis. Come on, Elvis, this way." I called and called, cajoling and imploring him, but he remained as if rooted to the spot. The water was very deep, too deep for Elvis to stand; he must have been balancing on a submerged rock or branch. A leaf and then an insect floated slowly past his muzzle, his poor huge soppy face peeping out of the water looked very vulnerable.

There was nobody else around, and he was too far for me to reach, but I was going to have to do something. I lay down on my stomach in the mud and tried to grab his collar. Too far away. I inched farther and farther over the bank, my upper body precariously balanced over the brown water, and somehow managed to grab his collar with my fingertips. I stretched some more, and then he stretched his neck up so I could get his collar in my whole hand. I grabbed it and then pulled and pulled and pulled, scrabbling backward on my belly. Elvis scrambled up onto the bank and was safe.

Once on land, he shook himself vigorously and river water splashed all over me.

"Thanks, Elvis," I said, and we trudged home. He seemed none the worse for his adventure; I was scraped and bruised and muddy but mainly very relieved that I'd managed to get him out alive.

Jamie came to pick him up later.

"How was he?" he asked.

"Fine, fine," I said. "Although Freddy's got a slight limp from keeping order and putting Elvis in his place."

"Make sure he has a good rest and a gentle day tomorrow," Jamie said, "and he'll be fine too."

Freddy was so exhausted he fell fast asleep on top of one of Ian's trainers. I didn't have the heart to wake him and move him to a more comfortable place, and so he slept on—on top of the trainer that was almost the same size as him—for most of the afternoon.

After I'd showered and changed, I found a message on my computer from my friend Susan in Ecuador. She was coming to visit the UK with her husband, Graham, and a surprise companion: Eliana.

"I took Graham to the orphanage so he could meet Eli," read the e-mail, "and he fell in love with her just like I'd done and so . . . we've adopted her. She has to be the most adorable little girl in the world. We're coming back to the UK so she can have specialist treatment at Great Ormond Street Hospital, so if you have the time it'd be great to meet . . ."

I definitely did have the time and I couldn't wait to meet Eliana again, and also to congratulate Susan and Graham about their momentous decision—which I could only see as being a fantastic thing for them all. I kept remembering how Eliana had made a beeline for Susan as soon as she'd walked in the door at the orphanage. It was as if Eliana had known, even before Susan did, that she was going to be her mum.

14

Two weeks had passed—weeks full of dog showers, intensive training at the Helper Dogs Center and a whole lot of fun and sleepless nights as Ian and I relearned the joys of looking after a brand-new pup and fell totally in love with him. Even on my worst days he could make me laugh. He was so entertaining. And it wasn't just me who could watch and play with him for hours. Ian was completely smitten too. There was something about how Freddy lived so completely in the moment that was very appealing. If it was food time, he gobbled up his food with gusto; sleep time, he was completely zonked out; and play, well, play needed every ounce of concentration.

The newspaper asked me to write up Freddy's diary for the column:

TUESDAY: FOOD

Today I finally managed to get into my full sack of puppy food and gobble up as much as I could before Meg caught me. She put pegs on the bag after that. But I managed to pull off the pegs. Now she's put the food out of my reach. It's not fair. I think I'm big enough to get my own meals when I'm hungry.

FRIDAY: TIDY PUPPY

Meg and Ian are very pleased with me because I am such a tidy puppy-boy. When I've finished playing with my toys,

I like to collect them all together and put them in a special round furry bed that's in the garden. I've got lots of toys. I especially like my pirate ball and my cow that goes moo.

SATURDAY

Fergus (Labradoodle) came to visit for the weekend. We went to a country park and I got to splash in a big puddle with Fergus. Ian wasn't too pleased about having to carry me back as I made him all muddy. But I'm only allowed to go on little walks at the moment so I have to be carried sometimes. Meg made us some special dog bones from flour and oats and meat—they were yummy. I barked to tell her I wanted a hundred but she only lets me have one each day.

Freddy was doing very well at Frank's obedience classes, where he was learning to sit and wait and not to take food off plates until I said he could. We had to put paper plates with dog biscuits on them on the floor, close to the puppy, with the stern command "Leave it!" and the puppies had to resist helping themselves. Mainly they managed it, although for some, especially those who'd had breakfast early, it was sometimes impossible.

Helper Dogs classes were going well too, barring one or two aberrations. If I popped out to get something from the car, Freddy wouldn't stop barking until I came back, and, once, Jamie had tried to put him in the crate at the center; I'd taken him outside and said, "Busy busy," the usual words for toilet time, but to no visible result. Then we'd gone back in.

"We'll just give him five minutes first of all and build it

up," Jamie said. It seemed like a sensible plan but no sooner had he put Freddy in the crate than he started barking. "Just ignore him," Jamie said. "He'll stop soon."

But Freddy didn't stop and began to wee in the crate to show what he thought of being shut in and ignored.

Jamie wasn't pleased. "What a naughty puppy," he said, letting Freddy out of the crate so he could clean it. Freddy didn't look even the slightest bit guilty.

All in all, though, he was a model pupil, and he'd been selected to perform at the Helper Dogs Summer Fête. Being the youngest, and incredibly cute, he had a starring role, following me and weaving in and out of traffic cones placed in a line. He did it perfectly in class, but I was still a little nervous about how he'd do on the day. I hoped he'd be able to concentrate, especially as it was the day that Susan and Eliana and Graham were due to visit. Susan had thought that Eliana would enjoy the fête: it was to be a little treat as she was going into Great Ormond Street to start her treatment the next day.

Finally, the big day arrived and they were at the door. I gave Susan, Eliana and Graham a big hug each in that order and then turned to feast my eyes on Eliana. She'd grown a lot and wasn't so thin, and her dark hair was even longer than it had been at the orphanage. She was still far smaller than she should have been for her age and needed a walker to help her move. Her smile was infectious.

"Wow!" I said to her. "Aren't you pretty?"

"Yes," said Eliana, her smile getting even bigger. She'd even started to learn some English.

"She's really, really bright," said Susan. I sat them all down and, forcing everyone to consume buckets of tea and cake, didn't let Susan stop talking until she'd explained everything that had happened in the eight months that I hadn't seen her—I'd been so busy that I'd been bad at keeping in touch on e-mail.

They'd been allowed to adopt Eli so quickly because of her special needs and because of the loving care and medical attention that Susan and Graham had promised. The prognosis when she was given to the orphanage was that she would never be able to do anything, but it had been clear to Susan that this was rubbish. They'd taken her to a specialist doctor as soon as they'd had legal custody over her, and with physiotherapy and the intensive work that they'd organized, she was developing quickly. The most serious problem was her hips, which had failed to grow properly due to her not being able to move about freely like other children, so they'd arranged a special consultation and corrective operation in London. Best of all, although she was still undoubtedly behind other kids her age, she showed so much enthusiasm and will to learn that her intellectual development was coming on in leaps and bounds.

"Remember the baby I was thinking of adopting?" Susan said, and I nodded. "She went back to live with her real mum."

This seemed to happen quite often in Ecuador. Being in the orphanage didn't necessarily mean the child was strictly an orphan or that the parents wouldn't take them back at some time.

Graham pointed to Eliana's new rolling walking frame in the corner of the room.

"There's been no stopping you since you had this, has there, Eliana?" He smiled at his daughter.

Eliana shook her head.

"She's making up for all those weeks she couldn't move at all, when she had that hip spica cast on," Susan said.

"What's that?" Ian asked.

"I called it the mermaid cast because she looked like a mermaid in it," Susan told him. "It was a fiberglass cast that encircled her waist and both her legs like a mermaid's tail so she couldn't move."

Eliana was tentatively patting Freddy, and he was keeping perfectly still so she wasn't frightened. She wasn't used to dogs and was a little nervous of him at first, even though he was still tiny. Luckily, she couldn't have chosen a better dog to get acquainted with. Susan lifted her onto her lap, and I held Freddy and let Eliana give him a few of his treats so that they could get to know each other.

As Susan and I carried on talking, Freddy brought over his blue dog toy to show Eliana. She began warming to him, picking up his toys and offering him them to pick up and play with. I told her all about Emma and how our lives had been changed by becoming puppy parents. Susan told us about all the physiotherapy Eliana had been having. It had been slow, painful work that had caused both her and Eliana to cry. They'd also paid privately for speech therapy, which had done wonders. They didn't know how far the little girl would be able to go, but they wanted her to have every chance of getting there.

"She loves swimming and is fantastic at it, like a little seal," Susan said. Susan and Graham were both enthusiastic swimmers and having a daughter who loved the water too was very good news. Susan smiled at a memory. "I remember Graham was away for a few days when I brought her home, but when he came back I asked him to keep an eye on Eli because she was in the bath and I needed to get a fresh towel. I came back and I could hear the two of them laughing together as she splashed about. I listened to them from the other side of the door with tears streaming down my face. It felt like all the years we'd had to wait were worth it now we had her. My mum always says the reason I couldn't have children was because we were supposed to be Eliana's mum and dad all the time."

I told Susan about our own difficulties and that we were thinking of going to a private clinic. Her experience of private clinics had been good and she advised us to go ahead.

Eliana crawled onto my lap and we played with the miniature crockery set I'd bought for her. She was still so small and fragile. One day, maybe one day soon, I'd be playing with our own daughter, I thought, hoping against hope.

"Tea, Meg, drink tea," Eliana said, holding out a cup to me.

Eliana made us all miniature cups of tea and then it was time to set off for the fête. Eliana walked behind her roller walker, with Graham shepherding her on the uneven grassy field.

That afternoon was Freddy's second fête, and this time he'd been vaccinated long enough ago to be allowed to walk on the ground. At the previous one, a couple of days after he came to us, he was too young to have had his second vaccination and so was at risk when in the vicinity of other unvaccinated dogs, but he was the only young puppy in training at the time and was so cute that Jamie, who was always on the lookout for new volunteer puppy parents, begged us to take him along. He'd looked funny in the special soft padded black dog bag that Ian had bought on the Internet, with just his snowy white head peeping out of the head hole. It must have been comfortable because at one point he took a nap, and a shocked passerby had said, "I thought that was a stuffed toy dog at first!"

"Oh, no, he's all real," Ian had replied.

Eliana, Susan and Graham found a spot close to the demonstration show ring while Freddy, Ian and I went off to join the other volunteers and their dogs.

There was a chorus of *ahhh*s from the crowd as Ian walked Freddy round the edge of the ring.

"Can my little boy stroke him, please?" one lady asked. "He's usually terrified of dogs, but he wants to touch your one."

Freddy was very good while he was stroked by the beaming little boy. "Mummy, I did it. I touched the dog," he said proudly.

Ian told me later that he'd heard Eliana say to her parents that she was going to get a dog just like Freddy.

"All the time she was saying this, Susan and Graham were shaking their heads." He laughed.

I laughed too. I reckoned a girl as determined as Eliana was would probably soon wear her parents down and have a dog eventually.

Jo was at the fête too, with an overexcited Elvis, who was doing his best to stretch his lead and charging around in small circles like a bull in a china shop. Ian agreed to take him for a while to give Jo a break. Soon it was time for

Freddy to take the center stage. Jamie had set up twelve traffic cones in a line across the grass and wanted the dogs to weave in and out of them on command.

"This is one exercise where the youngest dogs usually do much better than the older ones," he said. "Meg, why don't you demonstrate for us with Freddy?"

I took Freddy to the start of the line of cones, and when Jamie nodded at me, I started weaving quickly in and out of the cones. Freddy was right there behind me. He took no notice of the other dogs or all the people at the fête, sticking close to my ankle all the way along.

When I came to the end of the cones, I told him to sit and he immediately did so, as the crowd of onlookers clapped.

"What a good boy you are," I said, and gave him a treat.

"See if he can wait," Jamie said.

"Wait," I said to Freddy, and held up my hand, palm facing him, to show him exactly what I meant.

Puppies, like the toddlers they are, find it very difficult to wait. Their sense of time, and in particular their perception of how long they've been waiting, is at odds with that of the adults around them.

Freddy was still only twelve weeks old, and I thought he might find it very difficult, particularly because of the distractions of the people, dogs and the new environment all around him.

"Wait," I repeated, and started to walk backward through the cones, still holding up my hand. Freddy's eyes never left me once. I reached the end of the row.

"Come, Freddy!" I said in an excited happy voice, and crouched down, holding my hands out to him. He ran to me as fast as he could.

"Sit," I whispered. And he sat and looked up at me. As proud of himself as could be. He knew he'd done well.

"What a good boy," I said, crouching down to give him a cuddle and a treat. "Very, very clever!"

He was a talented little puppy; it was plain to see for everyone at the fête, but Jamie in particular was impressed.

Back at home, Eliana and Freddy played together with some of Freddy's many toys. She seemed to have no fear of him now and once or twice even gave him a kiss—which Susan and Graham didn't seem to think was a good idea. Freddy somehow seemed to realize that he needed to take extra care around Eliana and was very gentle. The day might have been overwhelming and tiring for them both, but Freddy was already showing that he liked to look after people, and

Eliana had become much more confident in the presence of another miniature being—and not just with Freddy but with everyone.

I caught Ian watching the two of them together and smiled at him. Maybe it was time for us to investigate the possibility of IVF further. We'd been so busy with losing Emma and gaining Freddy that it had taken a backseat.

15

Every day Ian had a two-hour journey on the train and tube to get to work, starting at 5 a.m. Then, in the evenings, he turned around and tubed and trained it home again. Usually, I'd drop him off and pick him up at the station, which some days was quite a stretch; whenever I suggested to him, though, that I might not do it, he'd tell me how important that extra ten minutes with me were to him, how it brightened up the dark grim mornings . . . so how could I refuse?

One night the week after Eliana, Susan and Graham had left, Ian phoned sounding exhausted. He'd had a nightmare of a journey—all delays and diversions—and had ended up at a small, isolated station. One of the many things I loved about him was his calmness in emergency situations. One night when we'd first started going out, we were so busy mooning at each other and staring into each other's eyes that the bag containing his work computer was stolen. This was a disaster because there was sensitive information on the laptop, and he'd had to phone his U.S. office immediately to explain the security breach. He'd dealt with each portion of the emergency with a calmness I'd never be able to achieve, leaving me full of admiration; so if he was at the end of his tether, he must have been exhausted after another long day of work and travel.

"Don't worry, I'll find the station," I said as he tried to explain to me the route I should take to get there.

I pulled some shoes on and grabbed the car keys. Freddy had been sitting at my feet while I worked on the sofa, but at the sound of the phone, he had begun prowling around the room looking for computer wires to chew on—his latest obsession—and currently appeared to be considering urinating in what had become his favorite corner of the room. He was too little to leave by himself for any length of time, but there was a problem taking him with me: I didn't have a car harness for him as I'd passed on Emma's, along with her princess bolster seat and all of her many other possessions, to Helper Dogs, and I was loath to put him in his crate that he hated so much. A rebellious puppy "accident" wouldn't make anybody's evening less stressful. Nevertheless, he had to come. Other puppy parents put their dogs in the front footwell on the passenger's side of their car when they were traveling, so I decided to try that. At first he sat quite still and it seemed that it might work, but as soon as I got onto the busy bypass he decided he wasn't going to sit still anymore and started clambering about and yapping.

"Calm down, Freddy. Stay still." I tried to soothe him, but his Helper Dogs obedience seemed temporarily to have deserted him; he wasn't at all frightened, just increasingly excited, and I was having a job keeping my eyes on him and also on the road.

"STAY STILL!" I barked, and Freddy, without paying me a blind bit of notice, stamped on the button that changed the car from automatic to manual transmission. At forty miles per hour on the dual carriageway the engine revs soared as the transmission struggled to cope. Quickly, fearing he'd kill us both if I didn't do something, I pulled over, screeched to a halt on the gravelly border and, kissing his nose as he didn't know he was doing anything wrong, very regretfully put him in the boot of the hatchback. I drove the remaining distance to the station both as fast as I could (to shorten the ordeal for him) and as slow as possible, terrified that he'd be injured because of not being strapped in.

I pulled into the small station car park and drew up in front of Ian's huddled figure. I pecked him on the cheek and ran around to open the back of the car. Freddy bounced into my arms. I hugged him to me; I'd never been more relieved.

"I'm sorry," I said. Sorry for being so stupid. It wasn't his fault he'd put us in danger.

Ian had been sheltering under an awning from the autumnal winds for over an hour and was very pleased to see us. He was exhausted from the terrible train journey, but Freddy soon cheered him up.

"We'll stop at the pet store on the way home and get him a harness," he said.

Ian drove the car home while I had Freddy on my lap. Freddy soon fell fast asleep after his adventure, and Ian and I took the time alone to talk about IVF once more. Seeing Eliana, and how happy Graham and Susan were, had made us both realize we'd still like to have a child of our own. Since their visit, I'd started to look into the practicalities again and had landed once more upon the clinic I'd found a few months previously, in Billingsford.

"I think this could be the answer," I said. "Susan got pregnant with three embryos once when she had IVF. Of course they didn't . . . they didn't survive."

It must have been about five years ago that Susan had

rung, from her mum and dad's, where she'd been staying, to tell me the news.

"They've put me on complete bed rest so all I can do is lie here and watch TV. But there's three—three!"

A week later Susan wasn't pregnant anymore. In more than ten years of trying it was the first and only time she ever became pregnant.

"They're having an open evening next week," I said.

There was the problem of the puppy, of course, and also that Ian wouldn't get home from work until just before it started, so we agreed that he'd stay and take care of the pooch while I went along.

The next morning, I booked my place for the open evening at the fertility clinic and then put Freddy's tiny Helper Dogs jacket on him and drove the short journey to the supermarket, using the new harness that Ian had bought on the way home from the station.

The idea of taking Freddy to the supermarket was to habituate him to new places, noises, smells and people, and to give him a first experience of one of the environments where he'd be expected to work. The little Helper Dogs coat he was wearing clearly said on the side "Helper Dog in Training" along with "Please do not disturb me as I am working." Some of the stricter puppy parents would tell passersby not even to stroke the puppy while it was working, but I found that impossible to do—and nobody we met could keep their hands off Freddy. At thirteen weeks old, he was utterly and totally adorable. His fur hadn't really settled down, as some puppies' did, and he looked, when freshly showered, as if he'd been through the tumble dryer or received an electric shock. He was always more than happy to let people stroke him and cuddle him.

I hadn't been able to forbid anyone to stroke Emma either, all too aware that, especially for children, it may be their first experience of stroking a puppy—and that a Helper Dog, with its sweet temperament and smart jacket, was a good dog to trust. Often, too, I'd meet people who were grieving a lost dog, and they'd want to stroke, chat and reminisce for hours. Walking around town with a Helper Dog pup always made me half an hour late for any appointment—and I was rarely on time to begin with. I'd found with Emma that shopping with a Helper Dog was trying when you needed to get everything done quickly, and with Freddy you could measure the time it took on a sundial. People couldn't resist coming to say hello and made a beeline for him down the aisles. Some even forgot about their own shopping entirely and followed us around the aisles. As he was still a very little boy, all the attention quickly got too exhausting for him. So much so that he lay down to nap in the middle of the supermarket.

"Ahhh, isn't he sweet," people said as they maneuvered their shopping trolleys around him, prostrate plum in the center of the aisle.

I was worried that someone might bump into him accidentally, so I abandoned my shopping plans—who needed food anyway?—and left my basket and carried him toward the exit. As I was about to leave, I saw the row of shopping trolleys and realized that here was the perfect solution. I popped Freddy into one of the smaller trolleys and went back to my basket, rescued the items and resumed shopping. Now he could take a nap, people could pet him and I could buy some food.

Freddy's trolley arrangement went really well and we became a regular attraction. One day we arrived at the store to find a mum and her two young sons standing outside. The boys pounced on Freddy as soon as we got there, while their mum sheepishly explained that, while they never used to want to come shopping, once they'd heard about the little dog in the trolley they'd become desperate to see him. We'd become part of local life: it reminded me of what one of the Helper Dog partners had said to me at the fête.

"I used to be too frightened to go to the shops. My joints dislocate really easily—just bending down to pick a tin off a low shelf can make my shoulder dislocate. I don't know if you've ever had a shoulder dislocation, but it isn't exactly a walk in the park," Mark had said. He was a man of about thirty-five who'd been given a Labrador called Tilly the year before.

"Then I got Tilly and everything changed. No one used to talk to me before, but now people want to chat to me all the time. Till is like my social bridge. Plus she loves going shopping! My life is a million times better because of her. She even hands over my wallet and helps put the shopping in my shopping bag. Since I've had her I haven't had a single dislocation—she's always there when I need her and she never lets me down."

Freddy rode around the supermarket for weeks, until one day we were stopped by one of the staff, a young, inexperienced man, who ran over and said that unfortunately the store had received some complaints about hygiene. I explained that he was a trainee Helper Dog and therefore allowed in the shop, to which the boy said that coming in was fine, but he wasn't allowed in the trolley.

I was furious. Which spiteful person had complained?

He was very apologetic, and really only a kid who must have drawn the short straw among his colleagues to tell me the bad news—I knew that Freddy was popular with all the checkout staff. But rules were rules, so I swept Freddy up and left the supermarket vowing never to go back.

Freddy found the regular market in the square, with its variety of smells, far more interesting, and, really, I reflected, he'd been so good at being in the supermarket anyway that there was no need to go back until he was a qualified Helper Dog, and far too big for any trolley.

16

I was driving along the motorway on my way to the IVF clinic's open evening and thinking of Susan and Graham. They'd gone to endless fertility clinics and endured years on different regimes of pills, injections and alcohol-free living while they were trying for their own baby, before they adopted Eliana. I said a silent prayer in the hope that it wouldn't take so many years of trying, before giving up, for me to get pregnant.

I had imagined the clinic would be part of a hospital, but it was in a very large house on a residential street, with just a small, subtle sign. It was near the general hospital and I wondered if perhaps it had been a convalescent hospital in the old days, the sort of place where people went to recover after they'd had a major operation. It was an Edwardian redbrick building with a metal spiral staircase at the back that descended into a small car park.

I arrived much too early and sat in my car, waiting and watching, as other people arrived. About half of the women seemed to be with their partners, who carefully helped them out of the car and into the building as if they were already heavily pregnant. Five minutes before the talk was due to start, I followed them in and was directed to a room with about thirty chairs. I sat at the back. People were well spaced out and weren't talking to or looking at each other. The atmosphere was palpably tense.

The talk began and everyone leaned forward in their plastic chairs, eager for any scraps of hope as the smart, middle-aged lady who managed the clinic told us about the procedures their doctors carried out and the high success rate they achieved. The eggs would be extracted and the embryos would be grown at the clinic; then the procedure to return them to the womb would be conducted there too, the aim being to cause as little stress as possible. She spoke eloquently about the facilities and the advantages they offered.

"Fertility treatment at a larger hospital might mean you don't know which doctor you'll be seen by from week to week. Here we have a small dedicated and professional team. You'll be treated as a valued individual. A member of the family, almost . . ."

There was polite laughter at this.

"And we like nothing better than when one of our clients pops in to show us how well the baby we helped them conceive is doing."

Then a male doctor gave us some statistics and told us the clinic's statistic for new patients who were under the age of thirty-six was more than double the national average. What about older women? I wanted to know, but I wasn't brave enough to ask.

After the talk we were given a tour of the clinic and shown the laboratory, scanning room, consultant's room and ward. It all looked very new and spotlessly clean, and I was impressed. It was small, but I hoped that small would mean I wouldn't be lost in the system, and they'd pay my tricky case some special attention. By the end of the tour, the atmosphere had thawed: couples were smiling and talking to each other. We were invited to stay for coffee and to ask questions, but I'd heard enough. I was sure this was the clinic for us. The atmosphere had been welcoming and professional, and their procedures seemed to work smoothly for the vast majority of people they treated. All we needed was some private treatment and I'd be pregnant in no time. I tried to book a private consultation for Ian and I there and then but was told I'd need to get some blood tests done at my local hospital first.

I drove home, excited and happy, to tell Ian the good news.

The next morning I took my temperature as usual and waited, lying back into my pillow, for the little beeping sound to alert me that the reading was ready. Freddy's familiar tread hit the stairs, and he came into the room and began pawing at the bed. Ian helped him up, turned to the mirror to finish knotting his tie and went downstairs to make some breakfast and bring me a cup of tea before he left for work—he was driving himself.

Freddy was delighted to be on the bed, and scrabbled and snuffled a bit but soon settled down for a cuddle. It was bliss. Warm and in bed, not being obliged to get up. Maybe a baby would come, maybe it wouldn't. Either way, I didn't have to think about it just now. Freddy jumped off the bed and went to investigate as Ian left. I heard the sound of the car driving away as the dog trod carefully down the stairs. He returned soon after and lay on the carpet as I dozed. Ten minutes more, ten minutes more . . . I awoke two hours later, just in time for a hospital appointment to confirm the blood tests I'd had for

Dr. Boston, which had shown I could possibly be a suitable candidate for IVF.

On the way back from the hospital, I stopped at the local shops for food and then went home. Freddy, whom I'd left shut in the kitchen, was very pleased to see me and hadn't done any damage while I was away, or gone to the toilet indoors. He helped me with the supermarket shopping by carrying one of the bags from the hallway to the kitchen. This was a surprise as I hadn't asked him to, and hadn't even been aware it was in his repertoire; his usual trick with plastic bags was to shred them with his teeth—which I found annoying and frightening in equal measure. This time, though, he took the bag—albeit a light one—in his teeth and gently deposited it with the pile in the kitchen. I was delighted with him and gave him a treat; my little boy was growing up.

The phone rang, and I went to answer it in the living room. When I looked around thirty seconds later, Freddy was lying on the sofa with a pack of raw chicken in his mouth. He hadn't tried to open it but had started ripping the paper off the back. I sighed. Oh, well. Some days it felt like we were taking one step forward and then taking two steps back.

Notwithstanding occasional lapses, Freddy was learning fast. Every day we ticked off another first: first swim in a stream, first oysters and shrimps consumed (at an oyster festival after his first trip on a train), first nap under a classic car (after eating shrimps and oysters). He was also coming on in leaps and bounds at his regular obedience class, led by Frank, and he'd made some great friends there, his

favorite being Morris, a Labradoodle, who was even boun-
cier than he was. He was patient and accommodating, even
as a puppy, and always ready to play, so he was naturally
popular even with cranky or antisocial dogs.

Another special mate of his was called Dodie, a Dalmatian whose breeder I'd met at Frank's obedience classes. She'd
been training her as a show dog—which meant Dodie wasn't
very good at her "sit" commands, because the shows involve
a lot of standing in position rather than sitting—but had
decided that she wasn't show material because she had a small
overbite. It felt heartless to me to consign an animal to the
scrap heap because of a barely noticeable physical imperfec-
tion, and I'd seen how Dodie would watch her and do exactly
as she asked almost before she'd asked her to do it.
Dodie tried so hard to please. So I arranged for a friend of

mine, whose elderly Dalmatian had just died, to take Dodie on. That way, Freddy was able to see Dodie at class and play with her down at the river, and both dogs were happy. Whenever Dodie came round, Freddy would let her gobble up any of his chews that she could find, and let her dominate their play together.

The longer he was with us, the more we became enchanted with him and his singular personality. Ian thought of Freddy as "his boy" and was always buying him toys and chews, and took Freddy on many more solo walks than he'd taken Emma.

Toward the end of Emma's time with us she worked out that she could get to the squeaky pad inside her toys if she chewed them enough; once she knew this, none of her toys were safe. Freddy, however, never tried to do this, and although he liked to play tug-tug with his toys, he never deliberately damaged any of them. In fact, he would often put them back into his toy box (a disused dog bed) himself when he had finished playing, and was very concerned whenever I put them through the wash or hung them on the line to dry in the sun. Nor did he like me repairing them with a needle and thread and would take them back from me as soon as he could. It was almost as if he was worrying that I might hurt them.

Freddy was like a young child about his playthings. Once, I'd gone out into the garden to find one of his toys, a spotty dog, balanced cowboy-style astride a small stone elephant that Ian had bought and which was placed in the corner of the garden. I laughed and laughed and laughed, and even phoned Ian to ask if he had put it there. He sounded confused, and obviously had nothing to do with it—he'd

been away at work since 5:30 a.m. It was all simply part of
Freddy's fun-loving nature, and I wondered whether he'd
done it on purpose, to make me giggle. He really was very
sensitive to people's moods.

Freddy was absolutely priceless that morning, as I gently,
without scolding, took the packet of chicken from his
mouth. I put it in the fridge and started to remove the rest
of the shopping from my carrier bags. Then I had to stop.
I put the tins down and started crying. It all seemed so
depressing and futile. I had left the house in such a sleepy
daze of optimism, but a few hours in Obstetrics were so
much more depressing after being at the IVF clinic, with
its clean, efficient promises of success and happiness. I'd
been floating on a cloud but came home feeling as if my
insides and my emotions had been put through a wringer.

I was still so far away from having a baby of my own.

Freddy jumped off the sofa and came through to the kitchen where I was standing, looking imploringly at me with his big brown eyes. He whined and then brought over a toy to me—I can only think to try and cheer me up. When that didn't work, he went to find another. Then another—this time, his favorite, a pink-and-white elephant—that he thought might work better. And, to top it off, a chew for me to gnaw on. I started to laugh and we ended up playing and cuddling. It was impossible to keep on crying when he was trying so hard to get me to stop.

Everyone who has a Helper Dog has stories of how their dog chases the blues away. A sad person often doesn't feel like leaving the house, but a dog eagerly waiting to go out is hard to resist, and a Helper Dog even more so—because after bringing over his lead, shoes will follow and, if they're ignored, a scarf and hat may come next. However, my friend Val told me that her Helper Dog, Saxon, had once sensed that she was going through a very dark time, and somehow knew to stay close and offer support.

"I don't know how he knew," Val said of Saxon. "But that day, I'd been told my prognosis was much, much worse than I'd initially thought and the pain was unbearable. I kept staring at the pills, thinking about taking just a few too many, and that day he never left my side once. He was right there, looking at me or cuddling into me. I swear he knew what I was thinking of doing, and I couldn't, I just couldn't, do it with him watching me with his big brown eyes. If it wasn't for him, I wouldn't be here. He's everything. I don't know what I'd do if I lost him."

17

Freddy grew very quickly and by the time he was sixteen weeks old was a lot larger than the other puppies at our Helper Dogs group, though he still had the long, loose-limbed look of a teenager. Only Queenie, quietly imperious in the corner, was bigger, and now that he deferred to her properly, she accepted his presence as she did any other dog.

In or out of the class, Freddy was very friendly with every dog he met and had the habit, which other dog owners admired, of sitting or lying down when he was off the lead and saw another dog running toward him—a polite way in dog language for a dog to say to another dog that he isn't a threat. But it takes two dogs to have a friendly conversation, and unfortunately for Freddy it didn't always work. One day, on a bright September morning on a walk in a large country park, I saw a man being dragged along in the distance by two very large St. Bernards.

"Come on, Freddy," I said, and headed toward them.

I wanted Freddy to have the opportunity to meet different types of dogs while he was with us. Socializing dogs with as many different breeds as possible can help stop them from taking against other dogs later in life. Sometimes, however, it's impossible for an owner to know a dog has a problem until a normally calm canine reacts in an extreme way, and although it rarely happens, Helper Dogs are not immune. At one of the Helper Dogs' fêtes, I'd watched a usually placid, fully trained dog, Yoda, suddenly run from his wheelchair-bound owner to bite a boxer, seemingly for no reason at all. Barry, the owner, was mortified and had no idea why Yoda would do such a thing. In this instance, as with all such cases, Helper Dogs worked with Yoda to overcome his aggression toward boxers.

I'd never met a St. Bernard before and neither had Freddy, so we went to say hello. The man, a rather slight fellow, almost dwarfed by his two heavyweights, was glad that we did. Most people were intimidated by the size of the St. Bernards, both male, he said, and consequently he felt nervous sometimes about letting them off their leads. I felt sorry for the dogs: how were they supposed to learn how to play with other dogs if they weren't given the chance? Helper Dogs recommends letting young puppies off their leads, in a safe environment, as soon as they've had their injections. I'd initially been nervous about doing so with Emma, but I'd learned that all puppies naturally want to stay close at that age; so I had relaxed with Freddy when he was a young pup.

"I took them to a puppy socialization class, when they were little—or at least younger, I mean," said Mr. St. Bernard, "but the guy in charge said they frightened the other puppies during off-lead time, and I had to keep them on their leads."

It must have been torture for them. Puppies have to play; denying them is like denying a child. I felt sorry for his dogs, and because Freddy was so good at playing and putting other dogs at ease I suggested they could have a go.

"Are you sure?" said Mr. St. Bernard doubtfully. "Maybe I'll just let this one off." He unclipped the lead of one of the St. Bernards, and the dog and Freddy began to play. They didn't look exactly comfortable, but I put this down to the big dog's lack of practice. The other St. Bernard, which was still on its lead, almost pulled the man over in his eagerness to join in.

Then, before I'd realized what was happening—maybe even before the dogs had a chance to realize what was going on—disaster struck. The first dog maneuvered Freddy in front of the second and the leashed dog bit Freddy, who gave a yelp of pain and ran off across the field. Without thinking, I grabbed the collar of the free dog. The man managed to clip its lead back on and yanked the two St. Bernards back in order. A police-dog handler I'd met at Helper Dogs had told me that if your dog is attacked and you put its lead back on while the other dog is still free, it is then even more vulnerable to attack from the aggressive dog, trapped and unable to move or defend itself freely. So I made sure the owner had his large, over-excited St. Bernards under control, and as soon as both dogs were secure, I called Freddy back from where he was standing, watching us across the long grass. Good boy that he was, he came, if a little hesitantly, back across the meadow. I couldn't see any serious injuries on him, so I decided it was just an unfriendly nip, and after saying goodbye to the St. Bernards, I immediately found some friendlier—smaller—dogs to play with for a while, to banish the bad memories.

Back at home, Freddy's breeder, Donna, popped around for a coffee. Freddy was very excited to see her and ran to find his pink unicorn to show her while I went into the kitchen.

"How's he getting on?" Donna asked.

"Great," I said.

"So he'll be moving on to advanced training soon?"

"Mmm." I poured milk into the coffees. I didn't want to think about that.

"My friend Marion is thinking of breeding her pedigree Golden Retriever, Sugar. You should phone her, Meg."

"But . . . I don't think we could deal with another dog on top of the puppy we're parenting."

"You could just go and have a look at them—it wouldn't mean you were committed, but if you didn't get in quick they could all be gone."

It didn't feel right to be looking at other puppies when we hadn't even had Freddy all that long. Freddy was gnawing on a chew beneath the table between us, smack bang in the center of the room, and center of my attention, even though I couldn't see him. It would feel like cheating on your husband—worse almost, since the victim was so vulnerable, innocent and blameless.

"But Sugar isn't even pregnant yet."

"No, but she will be soon and the sire Marion's thinking of mating her with has won Crufts. She's using the same sire that I used for Freddy. You could have Freddy's half-brother or sister. You should see the little girls Sugar has," Donna said, taking a swig of her coffee. "They're so pretty . . . These puppies are going to be very popular."

"All right, all right, I'll phone Marion," I said.

Donna read out the number from her mobile phone.

Marion answered after two rings and I confusedly explained to her my situation as far as I understood it—which wasn't far—tripping over my tongue as I groped obscurely for the words to express the twisted knot of emotions bound up inside me.

"You see, we've got a Helper Dogs puppy, but he's going to be moving on soon, and we're taking in another after, because they'll give us one when he leaves, and we couldn't take another puppy on top of that . . ." I trailed off. "But I'd love to come and see them."

"Oh, that'd be fine," said Marion. "You could come anytime, but I'm not sure if I should breed from Sugar at the moment. I've got such a lot on and the puppies will be ready to go to new homes just before Christmastime. It all seems too much."

I somehow felt like a blow had been landed to an ambition I didn't yet have.

"I'm sorry to disappoint you," Marion said as she put the phone down.

Donna, who had been playing with Freddy and his pink unicorn, suddenly gave a cry. "Meg!"

A drop of blood had fallen from Freddy and splashed red on the wooden floor. I rushed over to have a proper look. The St. Bernard's bite, which I'd presumed was just a grab, had cut deep into his chest. Freddy's mane of fur had soaked the blood up and most hadn't reached the surface, so I hadn't noticed. I felt sick; how could I have not seen how injured he was? How could I have called him back across the field when he must have been terrified, and then made him play with other dogs when he must have been in pain? Our poor little boy. How could I think about another puppy when I should have been paying attention to him?

I phoned Jamie to ask his advice and to get permission

to take Freddy to the vet's, and he said that if I bathed Freddy's wound with salt water he should be fine. Ian helped me bathe the wound over the next few days, but Freddy's long fur, which just soaked the water up, made the job difficult and soon it was looking worse. Jamie wasn't answering his phone, so I took Freddy to the vet anyway.

Sally the vet took Freddy away and shaved his chest. When she came back, I could see the large bite mark; some of the deeper indentations had become infected.

"Oh, Freddy," I said, feeling very guilty.

"It's a nasty bite," said Sally. I wondered if it could have been an accident from overenthusiastic playing, but Sally shook her head. It was definitely deliberate. The first dog may even have shepherded Freddy toward the second so it could attack.

Freddy was put on a course of antibiotics and the wound began to heal cleanly. Ian bought Freddy the largest chew I'd ever seen—longer than Freddy himself—as a get-well present. It made us laugh as it looked like a dinosaur bone next to our lanky little pup, and he never managed to finish it.

One of the dog walkers down by the river gave me a book with some recipes for convalescent dogs, and I dutifully made them for Freddy, who proceeded to wolf them down. His injury didn't seem to dampen his appetite at all.

After a few weeks, all that remained to show for the incident was a short patch of chest fur; after a little more time, that grew back too.

Fully trained Helper Dogs do sometimes have to deal

with attacks, and they're usually so devoted to their owners that they put their own safety second. One experienced older dog, Arthur, had been given extra sight training, as his owner, Stan, was blind as well as physically disabled and Arthur had been having a free play on a playing field when he was attacked by two other dogs. Although horribly injured and bloody from the mauling, Arthur had behaved heroically, going straight to his owner's side when called, so that Stan had been unaware that anything had happened until Arthur had safely led him all the way home.

Stan's wife, Fiona, had been horrified when she opened the door, she'd told me during a visit to our local Helper Dogs satellite center.

"I couldn't believe it. I felt sick. Arthur collapsed in the hallway, covered in blood."

"He lasted just long enough to see me home," Stan said, with tears streaming down his face. "Didn't you, boy?"

Stan patted Arthur, all healed, who looked at him adoringly.

"He put on three kilos during his convalescing with all the meals I made him," Fiona said.

Before we could get going at the private fertility clinic, I had to get my blood test results from my own doctor. I went full of optimism, but Dr. Boston gently told me that the results weren't just bad, they were awful.

"It's all right, don't cry," she said as a tear slipped down my face.

My hormone levels were much too high—I had very little chance of successful ovulation. If I didn't ovulate, then it was impossible to get pregnant. My FSH was now 18.7—it had rocketed up from last time, and my LH had gone up too.

I could hardly speak.

"But it's just—just we're so happy . . . A baby would be . . ."

The doctor handed me some tissues and put her hand over mine.

"I think you should consider donor eggs," she said softly. "Otherwise you may have more heartache and miscarriages because your eggs—if you ovulate at all—won't be good anyway."

I made it home but then e-mailed Ian at work, asking him to get a taxi that night rather than relying on me to pick him up. I didn't think I was up to driving. I then had a long conversation on instant messenger with Susan, who had returned to Ecuador with her family, to tell her what had happened. If anyone knew what I was going through, it was Susan. She was more than sympathetic. She'd experienced it all before.

"Years and years of tests and investigations. Tiny glimmers of hopes. Only to have them dashed."

I didn't want that. I wanted to have our baby naturally and easily—the way it should be.

"But did you ever consider having donor eggs?" I messaged.

"We tried donor eggs—that didn't work either."

It was getting late, and I had to give Freddy his food, put our own dinner on and a hundred other little household tasks that I simply couldn't face, so I had to sign off. Susan's final message gave me hope: she said that it didn't matter how you ended up with a child, the child was the important thing. "You're right: it's having someone to love," I messaged back, and shut the computer down.

The phone rang almost immediately. It was Marion. "I've changed my mind and am going to breed from Sugar."

"Oh. Oh, that's great," I said.

The next day Freddy went to visit Jo and Ian drove us to the fertility clinic. On the way, we talked Dr. Boston's advice over, and Ian said he would rather go for fostering or adoption than donor eggs. I was amazed. The idea of fostering and adoption appealed to me very much, but Ian had always avoided talking about it. I was concerned about him.

"What about if social services come and start digging around?" I said. If he could barely share parts of his childhood with me—or even himself—I feared for his reaction when outsiders asked him about it, and I could understand why they had a right to know their potential carers' backgrounds.

"I could tell them I was placed into foster care a few times," he said, making light of it. "It might even get us a few more brownie points in the interview." He smiled, but it turned quickly sad around the edges. He sighed. "To be honest, I can't remember anything about it, even though I did keep in touch with one of my foster parents until she died."

However much I tried to talk to him about donor eggs, he seemed not to want to consider it.

"It wouldn't be our baby," he said. "And I want it to be our baby with your eggs—not some woman's we don't even know."

I didn't agree with him, but he was adamant.

I crossed my fingers as we pulled into the IVF clinic car park, hoping that something would go right for us for a change.

The doctor at the clinic introduced himself as Peter Bromovich. He had a streak of mud on the shin of his trousers, food marks on his waistcoat, and a thick, unkempt beard, but he looked sympathetic and welcoming. I mentioned my bad results, and he said they may have been affected by the Clomid.

"What are you hoping to get out of the clinic?" he asked.

"I'd just like to know how good my eggs are," I replied, "to know if there's any chance of us ever having a baby of our own."

"We'll scan you on day five of your next cycle," he said, "but you must stop taking the Clomid now." Perhaps he saw the hope in my eye.

"I must be honest with you, the chances of a woman your age becoming pregnant using her own eggs is very slim— about one percent."

One in every hundred—that didn't sound too bad to me. Definitely worth a try.

"And that is pregnancy, not a live birth, which is obviously much lower. But if you opt for donor eggs, we could expect up to a thirty-five to forty percent success rate," he continued.

"I've no doubt there's one perfectly healthy egg inside you," he said. "And one day—in thirty years or so—we'll have something that will be able to extract that perfect egg, but at the moment we don't have the technology. Even if on the scan you produce a dozen or so eggs, which I think is unlikely, there's no guarantee that the eggs are good enough to produce a healthy baby."

Ian asked about the statistics again. He looked really worried.

"You seem concerned," said Dr. Bromovich.

"It's just . . . the chances using her own eggs seem so small, and there's so much to go wrong," said Ian. He turned to me. "If it doesn't work," he said, "you'd be so upset. I don't think you'd be able to handle it."

Standing there, in the clinic, on the edge of something very big, I didn't agree with him. In my mind, I protested: *I'm a tough old thing!* But as I continued to turn the problem over and over I started to change my mind. Suppose I did get pregnant, and then the baby growing inside of me died. I'd be OK, eventually, I thought, but the baby wouldn't. It would be awful. And Ian looked so upset and concerned. I swallowed hard.

"I think we should at least have the scan to see what's going on in there," I said.

"OK," said Doctor Bromovich, smiling gently. "You'll have to have some blood tests—HIV and hepatitis—first, and we have to charge for them. But seeing as we're waiting for your next cycle anyway, why don't you get them done through your hospital and bring us the certificates when you come for the scan?"

He showed us out, introducing us on the way to Jeannette, the nurse who'd perform the scan for me. She was a lovely, calm woman, and I immediately felt in safe hands.

Driving home with the top down, I found I was already

thinking about fostering seriously, and particularly about short-term fostering—where we'd get to look after kids in very short-term need, whose parents were in hospital, for example. If we tried fostering children for a weekend or a week, then it wouldn't be too hard to give them back and if we found we liked it we could go for longer-term fostering, maybe even adoption. Being over forty we were too old to be allowed to adopt a baby. But we would be allowed to foster one. Maybe if we were fostering a baby they'd let us keep it; I'd read about that happening on the Internet. I really wanted to have a baby. I wanted to hold a baby in my arms. In my head I knew exactly what I wanted to happen. We'd foster a baby and then its mum wouldn't want it back. And we'd get to keep it.

If I'm honest, I realized even then that Ian wasn't quite as keen on the fostering idea as I was, but if he didn't want us to use donor eggs then he was going to have to let us try fostering or adoption instead. Fostering seemed the logical first step and the process at the start was the same.

"I bet as soon as we stop thinking about having our own baby and go down the fostering and adoption route I'll end up getting pregnant," I joked.

We picked up Freddy on the way and arrived home as the sun was setting over the garden. That evening, on his laptop, Ian found the details of our local adoption and fostering service. The website warned that it could take up to a year to become a foster carer, but that was no reason to rule it out: nothing we'd done had been quick, and at least with fostering there was no biological clock ticking against us. I was watching television with Freddy and feeling sleepy when Ian came over.

"I've e-mailed them," he said. "They'll send us forms in five to ten days."

18

It was a blowy October morning, and I was braving a horizontal drizzle to try getting Freddy into the car. Freddy, though, wasn't budging. He didn't mind the rain at all and wasn't getting on with the front seat of my old Citroën anymore, so he was happy to stand in the road. His tail wagged slightly as he sniffed the air. At four and a half months old, he was too big to get up onto the high seat comfortably, or to perch there while the car was in motion. He had his car harness, but he certainly didn't need a pink princess bolster seat—he was liable to obstruct my view as it was. The previous week, he'd stumbled and fallen when jumping up to the seat, and now he was exercising his big-dog's prerogative and refusing even to try.

Given that we had an appointment to meet Jamie in town for a Helper Dogs progress meeting, it was all a bit embarrassing. Jamie was spending the day meeting each of his dogs and going on a walkabout around town to gauge how their training was going and to make plans for them to move on, but his star pupil, his first appointment of the day, was being decidedly disobedient and was threatening to scupper the schedule. Car-seat issues aside, Freddy was still learning fast, and I wasn't anticipating good news from Jamie—good news, in my book, being that I could keep Freddy for a while longer.

Ian, although at home, was on a conference call and so wasn't able to help me get the mutt in the motor. I called Jo, but she wasn't at home. I looked at my watch: it was a quarter to nine, fifteen minutes until my appointment. I was the first of the day and didn't want to make Jamie late from the start. It wouldn't go down well. I phoned another Helper Dogs puppy parent, Len, who lived nearby and who hurried around to help. Five minutes later he was packing Freddy safely into the car—the BMW, not the Citroën. We'd had a brainwave and decided to coax him into the other car. I'd protected the leather seat with a blanket, and Freddy had found the low-slung, luxurious convertible much more to his taste, as well as easier to get into. No way was I putting the top down to indulge him further, though. I was already wet enough as it was.

In no time at all, I was sitting in the convertible, Freddy looming beside me, starting the engine and ready to go.

"Thanks, Len,"

"No problem," he smiled. "I think sometimes dogs get themselves in a bit of a state—like children—and they need to be jollied out of it."

Jo hadn't arrived yet, but there wasn't time to wait for her. I drove off to the very dodgy-looking (but free) car park Liz had suggested we use, in our very expensive, never-to-be-left-in-a-dodgy-car-park car.

Jamie's Helper Dogs Transit van was waiting outside the car park—prevented from entering by the low barrier—as we arrived, so I parked up quickly and opened the passenger door for Freddy, like a chauffeur. Jamie put Freddy's lead on, cajoled him out and walked Freddy around a bit of scrub grass and said, "Busy, busy."

Freddy duly obliged, and then we were off. The river was flooded at the bottom of the grass, bringing all sorts of unexpected distractions, but Freddy walked incredibly well on the lead. He stopped and sat at each road curb and pedestrian crossing, and waited until Jamie said it was time to cross. He moved out of the way when people wanted to pass us. And he didn't have any "accidents" where he wasn't supposed to.

I was proud of my little puppy boy.

"What a good boy," Jamie said. "You've done a really good job with him, Meg."

"Oh, it wasn't me." I shook my head. "It was all him." I was feeling tearful anyway, but all of a sudden I also felt guilty that I hadn't taken Freddy to more classes, or to more nice places on long walks, with nice dogs. Unexpectedly, I also thought back to when, as a rangy pup, he'd been attacked by the bearlike St. Bernard. A tear slipped out of the corner of my eye.

"Hey, hey," said Jamie, "you did just fine. You did really well! He has the potential to make someone a great Helper Dog, thanks to you, and I'll be recommending him for advanced training as soon as he turns six months old." He smiled at me kindly before finishing: "Only you're gonna have difficulty letting him go, aren't you?"

Later, we met up with some of the other trainee Helper Dogs and puppy parents for coffee.

"Pants!" Jo said, bursting into the small coffee shop.

I didn't know what she was talking about.

"I'm sorry about Freddy," I burbled. "I just couldn't get him in the car. But then Len came and helped and I managed to put him in the convertible instead, and then I was late for Jamie and I thought I should just—"

But Jo wasn't listening. "I came around to see what was what, and your Ian was wearing his pants when I rang the doorbell!" she said.

I laughed for the first time that day. "They're not his pants—they're his loungey shorts, for when he's relaxing at home."

Jo sighed. "Well, I suppose I should be pleased that he'd got anything on at all," she said. "All I can say is there was an awful lot of flesh, Meg. An awful lot of flesh!"

At the end of the morning Jo took Freddy home in her car—a hatchback that Freddy jumped into with only a little encouragement. She'd parked on a side road, and drove me around to the dodgy car park to pick up my car. Thank goodness the convertible was still there and hadn't been damaged.

When I got home I told Ian what Jo had said.

"But they're my loungey shorts," he replied.

Then I told him what Jamie had said.

"Not Mr. Pup-Pup," Ian sighed as he stroked Freddy. "You can't leave us yet."

"What will we do? Do we want to be puppy parents or do we . . ."

"It's time we had one of our own," Ian said. "We need a forever puppy."

Though I'd consciously been skirting around the issue, locking my hopes and dreams into a little treasure chest at the back of my mind, I'd come to realize the same thing. Puppy parenting had been the best thing for us, the most amazing way to spend the first year of our married lives, but the wrench to give Freddy up was going to be so hard— too hard for us, maybe. It didn't get any easier with the second pup, loving them and letting them go, and nor did I think it would be the third, or the thirtieth, time. How could it be? Every puppy was so different, so vulnerable, so in need of loving: how could we not love them entirely?

Some people were able to love them and give them up for the good of the Helper Dogs' partners who needed them so much. I admired their ability to sublimate their own feelings and needs in favor of others time after time after time. I wished that I could keep on supplying beautiful well-trained puppies to Helper Dogs, creating a large extended family of dogs with grateful partners. But it was simply too painful for me: we simply weren't like them.

Maybe if our lives were different. Maybe if we were stronger people we could keep on doing it, helping Jamie and all the people who benefited from Helper Dogs. But for now all we wanted was a puppy of our own.

I began to dread telling Jamie that we didn't want to be puppy parents again. He was always so desperate for more puppy parents, and here we were thinking of letting him down. We probably weren't the best parents by a long way—far too lenient, and inexperienced—but we were sending good, bright puppies out into the world, puppies that would become loyal and faithful friends to their disabled partners. Both of our puppies had made it through to advanced training, which many puppies didn't do.

Then there was the question of my friends, who all seemed to be connected to Helper Dogs in some way and who'd all been so kind, and supported me every step of the way as Ian and I had tried to conceive. I didn't want to lose them, or for them to think we were abandoning them. Leaving Helper Dogs seemed like the best and most natural thing to do, but it also brought up conflicting emotions.

A week later, Marion phoned to tell us that Sugar was pregnant and we drove the forty minutes to the smallholding where she lived so we could meet the mother of our forever puppy.

Marion, a middle-aged lady with dark curly hair and rosy cheeks, greeted us warmly at the door, releasing a waft of freshly baked scones coming from her kitchen. Close behind Marion and desperate to be introduced were her three adult Golden Retrievers: grandmother Cinnamon, mother Spice and daughter Sugar.

"I usually only breed once from each bitch and then keep one of the daughters," Marion said.

Sugar was a doe-eyed beauty, large for a Golden Retriever, but with a very gentle temperament.

"Which sex puppy did you say you wanted?" Marion asked over tea and scones.

"A little girl," I said immediately.

Otherwise, we'd be comparing Freddy and the new puppy to each other. A different sex would mean she'd be accepted on her own merit.

Freddy was very excited to see us when we came back and very interested in the new doggy smells we brought with us.

We talked about our new puppy some more when we went to bed and were sure Freddy couldn't hear us.

"It'll be strange being able to name the puppy ourselves rather than calling it what Helper Dogs want to."

"We'll call it Trafford," Ian said.

"Trafford?"

"Yes, and one day she'll be Old Trafford."

I'd heard this Trafford idea before. Ian had suggested we should call our child by that name.

"It works for either sex," he'd said enthusiastically.

To me, it seemed much more fitting for a dog than a baby, and only marginally less silly than eating shepherd's pie every time Manchester United played (Ian thought it brought them good luck).

"OK—Trafford it is."

I fell asleep dreaming about our own puppy, our forever puppy, who'd stay with us until she was a very old lady. We'd never had a dog that stayed with us past their six-month birthday before. What a treat it would be.

19

All through Freddy's puppyhood, Helper Dogs had let us know every now and then how Emma was doing. In the first update, about a month after she left, we found out she was staying with a family with children, so she could experience a more boisterous, noisy life where she wasn't the center of attention. She had managed very well, and even resisted chasing after balls or trying to help remove socks and shoes during football practice. She'd have been good with our kids, if we'd had any, I thought when I read that the children she was with loved her, and that she was very gentle and patient with them. The truth of the matter was that she was good with everyone, and had become a firm favorite at the old people's home Jo used to take her to when she was looking after her for me.

It helped to assuage my guilt somewhat to hear that she was learning and developing, meeting new friends. I wanted her to be happy. I didn't want her to miss us, even though I missed her terribly. In my blackest moments I'd wonder if she thought she'd done something wrong that had made us give her up. Did she worry that her new people wouldn't love her enough to keep her either?

Even when Freddy was tiny and taking up every conscious moment, as well as intruding into my dreams and waking me up in the night, there was still time for me to worry about how our first puppy was doing as she made her way in the world, and to secretly ask for her forgiveness and understanding for having given her up.

After a few months, we heard Emma had been placed with Mike, a PE teacher in his early thirties who'd broken his neck in a motorcycle accident and sometimes used crutches but, on bad days, used a wheelchair. Often the information was very brief and came buried within e-mails about lots of the puppies. One simply said: "Emma and Mike's love affair continues."

Then we received the letter inviting us to Emma's graduation.

"She's passed!" I told Ian on the phone. "She's going to be a fully fledged Helper Dog."

Best of all, we were invited to the ceremony, which was to take place in the mansion at Helper Dogs HQ in Hertfordshire. We took Freddy with us.

Coffee and cakes for people and bowls of water for the dogs were waiting inside the mansion when we arrived, and we met lots of Helper Dogs and their owners before finding a place at the back of the very full graduation hall beside a man called Kev and his Helper Dog, a crazy Labradoodle called Scamp, with whom Freddy had played boisterously in one of the fenced-off grass areas before we went into the mansion.

"I think they paired me with him because I'm the only one who can keep up with him!" Kev joked, as he expertly maneuvered his extra-light sports wheelchair over the grass, but it was easy to see that Kev and Scamp totally adored each other.

With only five minutes to go before the ceremony started, I still hadn't seen Emma, and if I wasn't already nervous enough, I started to become anxious. Sometimes, if the Helper Dog's partner was ill, or found it too difficult to travel, then the dog didn't come to the center and their graduation was delayed to the next ceremony. Often this happened at very short notice. I hoped that this hadn't occurred with Emma. Then we saw her, with a man who must have been Mike, walking from the back of the room down the center aisle and taking a seat near the front. She was much bigger than when we had her, a real adult, and her coat had darkened. She didn't take her eyes from Mike once.

I followed their progress and realized that my arms had come out in goose bumps and that I was getting a bit dizzy from holding my breath involuntarily.

"Shall we go and say hello?" I said.

"Not now, the ceremony's about to start," said Ian, shaking his head.

So we waited, and the show began.

Each Helper Dog and partner came to the stage in turn and were introduced. Then the owner told the audience about their life before and after the dog. Some of the dogs were placed with disabled people who needed carers to support them, some with people in charge of their own families, and some with people who were living with their parents. Male and female, old and young, and from all parts of the country, they were united only by their love and gratitude for their Helper Dogs.

There were lots of heartrending stories as well as a few funny ones. One young man, Matthew, took to the stage, and described his life living at home with his mum and dad.

"I need a lot of physical help, and I was so desperate for

a dog I was phoning the Helper Dogs office twice a day some days," he said. "In fact, they rang my mum to ask her to tell me to stop: 'We'll let you know straightaway when there's a suitable one!' they said." He blushed. "But I just borrowed my mate's mobile to ring them instead. Now I've got Dailey, he's transformed my life.

"He just does so much that I hadn't expected. I was delighted that Dailey can open drawers," he continued. "Because of my condition I don't have the strength to do it myself, but with a bit of rope and a ball attached to the drawer Dailey does it with ease. I don't like drafts—my hands swell up and turn blue in the cold, and he can open and shut all the doors in the house. When I get really cold, he brings me a blanket and cuddles up to me to keep me warm. He's always so gentle and careful. It's as if he knows this body of mine should have a 'fragile' label attached to it."

In fact, Matthew hadn't chosen Dailey; Dailey had chosen him. The bond between a Helper Dog and their partner must be much stronger than that between a person and their pet, so Helper Dogs' usual procedure is to take a group of people wanting dogs, people who've passed the assessment and have suitable living arrangements, and put them in the same room as the latest batch of trained puppies. The center staff then look on as the humans and dogs get to know each other and the dogs naturally gravitate to their favorite people. Though it didn't always work perfectly, more often than not that particular person would end up becoming the dog's partner.

The next person on stage was a boy of twelve called David, one of the lucky few children that Helper Dogs worked with. Alongside his mum, Aretha, he showed the audience a video of what his dog, Connor, did to help each day. It started with Connor on David's bed and then David pretending to wake up and Connor licking him. Connor then brought clothes over to David, item by item, before giving him his towel after David had his morning wash. At school, Connor carried David's books in a special backpack and they were greeted by lots of friends as they walked down the corridor together. Then, in the classroom David dropped his pencil on the floor and Connor picked it up and put it on his desk before having a little snooze. He must have been dreaming about something nice because his tail wagged to and fro as he slept.

All through David's school day Connor was there, helping him. He even handed over David's money and got his change for him in the canteen. After school the two of them played and watched TV before finally going to bed.

"And that's our day," David said at the end of the video. "A day in the life of me and my best friend."

I loved all the stories, but I was desperate for our girl's turn. At last, Emma led Mike on to the stage.

"I first met Emma at the Head Office. She came running over to me straightaway. It was like as soon as she saw me she knew I was the one for her," he said. "Then they brought her to visit the school where I work and I was amazed how calm she was during a PE lesson—most dogs would have started chasing balls or barking at the kids.

"She's like my shadow, and I can't imagine what it would be like not to have her in my life now. She picks up my stick and my keys and takes off my socks, hats and gloves, which is really useful in the winter when I have three or four classes outside every day. One time, I was explaining something to the kids, they were all sitting down on the floor in front of me, and I saw out of the corner of my eye Emma, sitting at the end of one of the rows, with her head cocked to one side, looking like she was taking it all in. And I'm pretty sure she was—she's absolutely the smartest dog I've ever known. Sometimes, when I'm pointing to the kids during matches, she thinks I need her to fetch something and is there before anyone else has worked out what I was asking. She's so finely attuned to what I need that she's almost too clever."

Then the master of ceremonies asked all the people involved in Emma's life prior to her being placed to come to the front, one by one. My heart leaped as, being her first puppy parent, my name was first on the list. I made sure Ian had his camera out and then started the long walk to the front of the hall. I said hello to Mike, but I only had eyes for Emma, and could barely stop stroking her and saying hello. Finally, I straightened up, a little embarrassed at how long I'd spent catching up with Emma in front of so many people. The master of ceremonies started calling out more names, and I looked down at Emma once again. She looked up at me and then suddenly jumped into my arms for a cuddle.

"Sorry, sorry," Mike said. "She never usually jumps up."

"That's OK," I said, beaming. "She's remembering when she was a very little girl."

Emma's tail didn't stop pumping from side to side, and I couldn't have been more delighted.

We all had our photo taken with Emma, everyone who'd loved and supported her, and worked so hard to turn her into the dog she was today; then our moment was over, and I left the stage and went back to sit down with Ian and Freddy.

After the ceremony, lunch was served in a long, airy room looking out over one of the lawns, and I had a chance to chat with Mike and have a proper cuddle with Emma. Ian, too, said hello to our little girl and, gaining Mike's say-so, gave her a few treats for old times' sake. Mike fed her some curry from his plate, on a little bit of naan bread, and I smiled as I remembered how much she'd loved tasting our curry when she was with us. Even though we'd been asked not to treat the dogs as pets we hadn't been able to resist spoiling her a little bit, and it didn't seem to have harmed her at all.

"She so loves you," I said to Mike, totally approving of her being given yummy bits from his plate.

"And I love her," he said. "I was devastated just after I received her because I thought I might have to give her up again. I couldn't fit all her feeding and toilet schedules into my school timetable, but Helper Dogs was really understanding and said it could be adjusted to suit us both."

I stroked Emma and she stretched up her head for more.

"The other weird thing was that when they introduced all the dogs they said she was one that didn't need that much affection," he continued.

I looked at him aghast. "They did? Why would they say that?"

He shrugged his shoulders. "I don't know. I guess because she would still do what you asked her even if you didn't give her any affection."

I was so pleased she'd been placed with him and his

family, who were obviously showering her with affection, rather than a person who thought she didn't need it and so wasn't giving it.

"Don't worry yourself!" he said. "Every night she comes in to have a cuddle with me and my girlfriend, before going to sleep in our daughter's room, next to her bed."

She'd become an instant hit with everyone at school, and all around the small town in which he lived too. Once, he'd left her with a couple of trainee teachers for the morning, and had returned to the staff room to find a miniature obstacle course set up, with crisp crumbs beside many of the small jumps. The two students guiltily confessed that they'd made an agility course for Emma; then, as they got carried away in their tale, they forgot they were supposed to be acting contrite.

"She was really fast!" said the first.

"And she got even faster when we used the crisps," said the second.

"She could be like, like, a champion!"

"She's already a champion to me," Mike told them.

Emma and Freddy were overjoyed to see each other and had a long play together on the grass outside while we watched, smiling. Our two puppies.

When we left, I gave Mike a little photographic diary I'd had made of Emma's first six months with us, the cutest photos I could find along with extracts from her blog and her columns.

"If you ever need anyone to look after her for any reason . . ."

"We could always do it," Ian said. "We could even pick her up."

"Thanks," Mike said. "The Helper Dogs' support team usually sorts out that kind of thing."

It was time to go home.

"Bye, Emma," I said, and gave her a hug.

"Bye-bye, puppy girl," Ian said, and gave her the last of the treats we had.

Freddy kept looking back at her as we headed for the car.

I felt happy on the drive home. Emma was in the right place and with the right people for her. She helped Mike get on with his life, to complete all the daily personal tasks he needed, which allowed him in turn to teach all the kids that needed him. Without her, the school would have had to hire another PE teacher and he would be at home, feeling depressed and unwanted. I realized that I wouldn't have wanted to take Emma away for any reason, although if she ever needed a retirement home our house would always be there for her. Later that evening, Mike e-mailed to tell us his little daughter had taken Emma's diary to bed with her to have read as a bedtime story.

A few days later, Freddy breezed through his Bronze Kennel Club exam—lying down and staying down during his one-minute stay, coming immediately when he was called, resisting the other dog distractions and treats on the floor when asked to do so. The examiner was so impressed she suggested he try for his Silver exam too—even though we hadn't really practiced for it. Two exams in one day, however, was simply too much, and an overexcited Freddy chewed on his lead, pooed on the pavement and didn't jump up into the car when asked.

The examiner smiled as she shook her head: "Not quite ready for his silver yet," she said.

Nevertheless, the time for Freddy to move on was coming ever closer.

20

It seemed to take me weeks to get the house and garden spotless for the social worker's visit to talk about becoming foster parents, and the stress began to get to me as I worked like crazy making each room beautiful by turn. Ian worked from home the day before to give me moral support, but by that time I was feeling very fraught and his presence actually did the opposite. He said something in a funny tone of voice, and though I managed not to cry in front of him, I went straight out into the garden, burst into tears and cried so much that I couldn't talk to my mum when she phoned. Ian had to explain to her, and then to Jamie, who rang to find out why I hadn't come to class, that I was feeling a little fragile. Jamie told Ian to buy me a big cake, which finally stopped the flood and made me laugh. Jamie loved cake—it was his answer to most of life's problems.

I began to calm down.

"It makes me feel so hopelessly sad when you're mean to me," I told Ian, though I could tell from his face he had absolutely no idea what he'd done wrong. I wasn't even sure myself.

I carried on gardening outside for most of the day so he couldn't upset me more.

The next morning, I had a surprise visit from an old friend, Narinder, whom I hadn't seen in more than ten years.

Freddy, for some reason, was wildly excited to see her and she did very well—for a cat person—confronted with a huge bouncy puppy.

I hadn't known before her visit, but Narinder and her husband had tried to conceive for fifteen years without success. Then she'd had a massive heart attack. It was so touch and go that her family had been asked to come to the hospital to say their farewells, but she pulled through.

"After that we decided we were fine with just the two of us and our cats," Narinder said.

I told her about the social worker's impending visit. One of Narinder's sisters was going to be starting fostering training after a tough initial interview, and her mother privately fostered a boy with autism every other weekend to give his parents a break.

"She loves it," Narinder said. "He's like the grandchild she's never had and is never likely to have—at least not a birth grandchild."

Ian arrived home, smart and responsible in his suit, just before the doorbell rang for the second time that day.

"Oh, you have a dog," said Hazel the social worker primly when she saw the toy bones and teddies piled neatly in the corner. She was using the sort of voice usually reserved for cockroaches, or an infestation of moths.

"He's just a puppy," I said reassuringly.

Freddy bounded into view and she took two steps back.

"He's huge! I thought you meant a little puppy," she said. "I don't really like dogs," she added, somewhat unnecessarily.

I shut Freddy in the kitchen, but he got upset and started to bark, so I put him on his lead and he lay at my feet staring at Hazel, who'd sat in his favorite spot on the sofa. It was new, and he'd taken to sleeping upon it, his head resting on the arm. He tried to join her once or twice, but I held his lead close very tightly.

Hazel kept on shifting awkwardly, rearranging herself and her things, and glancing over at Freddy, which made us very uncomfortable too. She shuffled her papers, and opened and shut her folder while we tried to tell her about our experiences of working with kids with learning difficulties, and about both being Camp America counselors at different times. Ian had also just started reading with kids at a local primary school during his lunch hour, through a work corporate social responsibility scheme.

"Are you interested in fostering teenagers?" asked Hazel.

I looked at Ian. Although we knew some lovely teenagers, it wasn't something we'd really considered and I didn't think we'd be much good at it. Even with his dog-sized intelligence and capacity for mischief, Freddy walked all over us, so I was pretty sure it'd be a breeze for a teenager to do the same.

"It'd probably be best to take two children," said Hazel. "Siblings, I mean."

Now it was Ian's turn to look over at me.

"Maybe you should just try us with one first," he smiled nervously.

I showed her around the house, feeling very proud of how beautiful it looked, explaining how I'd like to keep my office, where I wrote, if at all possible. I showed her some of the picture books I'd written, feeling sure that this would clinch the deal—that we'd simply scream out "YOUNG CHILDREN" to her. Freddy, still on his lead, had calmed down and was being a good boy; I was radiating stressed-out vibes and Golden Retrievers are very intuitive.

"I'm not sure you could fit two kids in the back bedroom, unless you put the bunks around like that . . ." Hazel's voice trailed off as she mentally measured out the space. "Maybe an older child in here and then a baby in with you in the master bedroom. Listen, I can't say more now. I'll talk to my manager when she comes in on Friday."

She'd clearly had enough of Freddy and left. We had a celebratory glass of Cava, though we weren't sure exactly what we were celebrating, if we were celebrating, or even if she'd heard anything we'd said.

"She didn't seem to listen to our experience of working with kids with learning difficulties," I said. We'd thought that being interested in fostering children with special needs would strengthen our case.

"She definitely didn't pay any attention when we said we only wanted one child," said Ian.

The whole meeting had put a sour cast on the idea of fostering. In the space of an hour it had changed in my mind from a rich and personally fulfilling social service to something fraught with hazards. Hazel had repeatedly mentioned how many children had very challenging behaviors, and had said to Ian that even though a baby might seem easier to look after, foster parents usually had to allow the birth parents access every day, which might mean that an adult with drink, drug or mental health problems would be coming round to our house. I didn't like the thought of that at all.

But I wasn't ready to give up yet. This had only been the initial fostering meeting and I so wanted to experience raising a child with Ian. Hazel might have been having an off day, and surely, I thought, it was their duty to paint the blackest of pictures in order to weed out people who shouldn't be fostering. If we fell at the first hurdle, then it was right that we shouldn't be allowed to raise a child—the most important job there is. Besides, I wasn't going to let a snooty social worker put me off. We'd already been through so much at the hospital and at the IVF clinic. We were tougher, far tougher, than that.

At our next Helper Dogs class I told the other puppy parents how it had gone. Liz said a friend of hers fostered teenage girls.

"They can be complete terrors," she said. "They know exactly how to manipulate adults to get what they want, and there's not much a foster parent can do if they misbehave—you have no authority. The biggest punishment you can give is to take away their allowance, but you have to return it all as soon as they behave again."

I looked at the dogs. Freddy was playing with Finn, Liz's latest puppy. Finn was a week younger than Freddy and had been donated by a farm. When Freddy and Finn got together it was like two teenage boys having a scrap, and they'd been told off by Jamie more than once for misbehaving. I didn't tell Liz, but I was pleased that someone like her—a far more experienced dog owner—sometimes had no control over her puppy either. Elvis, meanwhile, was lying in the corner looking idly at the wall. At ten months old, he was twice the age of all the other puppies in the class, and his inclusion was more or less token; Helper Dogs had accepted he wasn't made of quite the right stuff and were investigating other options for him.

Len piped up from the corner, where he was with his little puppy, Gertie. She was just with us on a temporary basis because her puppy parent over at the Peterborough satellite was having a family emergency.

"I have some friends who foster privately for an agency, and they reckon that the district next to ours has too many babies and not enough foster parents at the moment," he said.

My ears pricked up.

"I'll give them your telephone number," he said.

"You don't want a teenager, Meg," said Jo. "You want a baby."

I knew that she was right.

Later that week, Jamie rang to tell me the news I'd been dreading: Helper Dogs had decided Freddy's fate. He would be going to a new puppy parent, Rachel, who lived about an hour away in a big farmhouse with a Labradoodle called Gandalf. Gandalf was a little older than Freddy; it was felt that Freddy would benefit from not being the center of attention all the time. It was also a good idea to move them on, Jamie had told us, so that they didn't become too attached to one person, as Dylan had done, and therefore be unable to bond with their final, most important, owner— the Helper Dogs partner.

Labradoodles like Gandalf were also occasionally employed as Helper Dogs, though they could sometimes be a little harebrained. Goldendoodles tended to be calmer and were becoming more popular. The advanced trainers at Helper Dogs HQ, however, tended to favor Labradors, or Labrador mixes, as they adored food and worked very well for treats. Golden Retrievers were a bit more intuitive and sensitive, and were more likely not simply to follow orders and to think for themselves. This was both a good and bad thing: good when they used their intuition and sensitivity to do helpful things; bad when they decided they didn't want to do something. Golden Retrievers could be very stubborn.

I decided that to try to head off the heartache I'd felt when losing Emma—because it had really felt like a loss—I'd become more involved in Freddy's move. I asked Jamie to give me Rachel's details, and I gave her a ring to arrange a visit for me and Freddy, so that I'd have some idea of his new life after he left me. Talking to her gave me a lump in my throat, and even as I put the handset down I questioned my own actions: was I just stretching out the loss, instead of diminishing it?

Too late to worry now, I thought, as I typed her postcode into the car's GPS. Her house was deep in the countryside, but perhaps as a subconscious revolt—a sly attempt to sabotage my own good intentions and keep Freddy with me for a while longer—I hadn't really listened to her description of where it was or how to get there. Freddy was being unhelpful too. He'd got used to traveling in Ian's BMW and now really objected to the high, cramped seat in my car. He didn't want to get in, and I was having real trouble persuading him because I didn't want him to either. I wanted to lead him back into the house, lock the front door and never come out again. He could sense my tension and reluctance, and decided to be obstinate.

"Come on, Freddy, in you get," I said, slapping the car seat to show him what I meant, knowing that he knew exactly what I wanted him to do. Freddy stood immobile, staring up at me.

"Come on." I tried to keep the desperation out of my voice, but of course Freddy could hear it, and suspecting I was trying to lure him to the vet's, the grooming parlor or somewhere as yet unknown but equally anathema to dogs, he now really didn't want to get in the car at all.

"Get in!" I said firmly, and, deciding to employ both carrot and stick at the same time, pulled a treat from my pocket and jiggled it in front of him. It was some sort of tripe stick, manufactured from unspeakable animal parts, and therefore one of his favorites. Reluctantly, begrudgingly, he deigned to climb in.

"I hope you're not tricking me," his expression said. "I don't like this car, I don't like the vibes you're giving off and I'm only doing this because you're my mum and I trust you." Which, of course, made me feel even worse.

I felt like crying, and not just for Freddy, but for Emma as well. Even now, if I so wanted, I could easily torment myself by thinking about Emma, but at least she was happy and loved with Mike. And now I was going to betray Mr. Pup-Pup in exactly the same way. Yes, today we were only visiting, but it still felt like I was rehearsing a betrayal. Today wasn't permanent, but even so I had to force myself to start the engine and roll the car off down the road.

About forty miles in, the GPS lost its signal and all of a sudden I was on the B road to nowhere. I had the address, but all I could see were fields, and in another act of self-sabotage I'd forgotten to write Rachel's number down. It all seemed so hopeless. I called Ian and cried down the phone while he looked up the way on his computer; but I wasn't in a fit state to take in the directions and then Freddy began to agitate to get out of the car. I said a tearful goodbye, and Freddy and I went for a long walk up the isolated lane, far enough to see that there were no signposts in the vicinity, nor any signs of life. Even so, I felt much calmer for doing something as normal as walking my pup. Freddy fell out once again as he was trying to get back into the car, which only made everything worse, but finally, as I was ready to turn round and head for home, the GPS miraculously recovered and we were on our way again— from one crisis to the next, or so I felt.

We arrived—me red-eyed, Freddy restive—at Rachel's an hour late. She brushed aside my apologies with a smile and made a huge fuss of Freddy. She seemed a kind, kind lady, with lots of long blonde curly hair, wearing hippyish clothes. I thought to myself: "I really want him to be with someone who'll love him more than anything." I realized it didn't bother me if he never did what anybody asked him ever again; if I had to lose him, I just wanted him to go somewhere he'd be loved.

Gandalf was also very pleased to see Freddy and immediately took him on a tour of Rachel's huge, orchardlike garden. They were soon jumping all over each other, barking and playing furiously, and Rachel, looking a bit worried, suggested we go for a walk in the woods to tire them both out a bit. As we did, we chatted and chatted and chatted, and I felt I'd made a new unexpected friend. Rachel, a widow who'd brought up three children on her own, was a survivor.

Back at the house, I decided that Freddy and Gandalf,

who'd been playing with each other ceaselessly since they'd met, should probably have a break.

"Gandy never seems to get tired," said Rachel, but I knew Freddy did, so we gave them each a chew, separated them by closing the door and opened a bottle of wine to give ourselves a break too. The two dogs were such good friends already that we had Gandalf whining and barking at the passage door and Freddy scratching at it to be let in as an accompaniment while we sipped our Prosecco. I accepted a second glass, and then another, thinking that I could get a taxi home and come to collect the car the next day. Then we opened another bottle, and by the time Ian arrived in a taxi from the station (I didn't entirely remember making the call), I was feeling very merry, and happy that, if Freddy really had to go, he was going to Rachel's. Freddy and Gandalf hadn't stopped playing, and I was slightly worried that having two teenage boys together might be awfully hard work for her.

Freddy had collapsed into sleep on the backseat as soon as we drove off, snoring and twitching every now and again as he chased Gandalf in his puppy dreams. I smiled at Ian. We loved watching our puppies sleep and imagining what they might be dreaming about.

Back at home there was a message from Marion to say that Sugar had given birth to eleven puppies, so I gave her a call and we arranged another visit so that we could finally meet them.

Ian drove us to Marion's smallholding after work a few days later and she took us straight through into the warm farm-style kitchen, where the puppies were together in a large crate with soft bedding next to the Aga. They clambered all over each other, making tiny mewling sounds. Blind, eyelids closed, with tiny pink-veined ears and the softest of soft creamy-colored coats. Their paws were huge compared with their bodies. Sugar looked at us with a combination of pride and concern as we cooed over her litter.

"She had eleven," Marion said. "But only three of them are girls."

"They're beautiful." And vulnerable, so defenseless. How could anyone not want to take one home and love it? But how could anyone take a puppy away from its mum? How could Marion be prepared to let any of them go? I was sure that the pain of separating from a pup would never get any less, no matter how many times it happened.

"Do you want to hold one?" Marion said, as she reached into the box.

She reached for the smallest of the puppies. Thinner than the others, she had a yellow spot painted on her back. The puppy mewled and squeaked in protest at being picked up. Marion gave it to me.

"It's one of the girls."

I held the tiny warm body close and the puppy nestled into me, still making a racket. A noisy girl—just what I wanted. This puppy would bark and let us know what was going on. This puppy would never stand out in the rain in silence waiting to be let in as one of the dog walkers at the river had told me his dog did.

"Would you like to hold one too?" Marion asked Ian, and he took another of the puppies into his arms. A gentle smile of pleasure lit up his face.

"We're going to be calling our puppy—that little one—Traffy," Ian told a surprised Marion, who hadn't expected us to have a name already, for this to be such a foregone conclusion.

"It's short for Old Trafford," I said.

21

I awoke the morning after visiting Traffy feeling guilty about Freddy. It wasn't the first time, but it was certainly the sharpest pang yet. He hadn't even left us and already we were thinking about the forever puppy that would be replacing him.

"She'll be able to wear Freddy's Manchester United shirt when the match is on," Ian joked, as he set off into the dawn to work. Freddy had grown much too big to fit into the special doggy football shirt Ian had bought him. Ian still considered him a Man U fan, and it was true that Freddy did still like to watch the matches; mainly, I suspected, because Ian gave him a Schmacko treat every time his team scored a goal—and Freddy was very fond of Schmackos.

"I feel so guilty," I said.

"Poor Mr. Pup-Pup," said Ian. We loved Freddy so much and were going to miss him at least as much as we'd missed Emma. Every day one or other of us would pipe up hopefully, saying maybe Helper Dogs would decide not to take him after all. Deep down, we knew it was wishful thinking: we both knew we couldn't keep him, however much we wanted to. We'd already been down that road once, with Emma.

"He'll have a lovely time at Rachel's. You know he will," said Ian.

I had to agree. There were woods for him to run in right next to her house, and Gandalf to play with, but I still didn't want to let him go. Although he was now huge, he was still our little boy, and we wouldn't be able to replace him.

"It's only natural not to want to give him up," Ian tried to console me, "but you know we can't keep him. We're Freddy's foster parents not his forever ones."

"I'm going to miss him so, so much," I sniffed.

"Well, maybe he won't pass. Maybe he won't be suitable as a Helper Dog and we'll be asked to take him back."

But it felt wrong to wish that. Freddy had more of a quirky personality than Emma and wasn't always so eager to do everything he was asked to, as Emma had been, but if you asked him in a nice voice (which I always did) then there was no stopping him.

"Supposing we'd never had a dog," Ian said.

"That'd be terrible." I didn't want to be dogless ever again. Life just felt right with a dog in it. Not to have one would be all wrong.

Following Len's advice, I'd contacted his friends, Nora and John, and they'd put me in touch with Parenting Partners, a private adoption and fostering agency. Kirsty, the lady who'd answered the phone, had been really nice and chatty. She'd asked all sorts of questions and she seemed to listen carefully when I told her about our previous caring experiences. She'd e-mailed afterward to say it had been a pleasure to chat, and that she'd send us all the forms and arrange a visit.

The next step for us was to invite Nora and John around to dinner and hear about their experiences of fostering over big warming plates of fish pie followed by apple crumble. To them it was a full-time job and hard work.

"You get paid more by the agencies than the council . . ." John said.

We weren't interested in the money side of it. Never had been.

". . . but the kids are usually more damaged—they're ones that the council couldn't place with regular foster parents."

"We have meetings once a month and are monitored and given counseling," Nora said.

She saw Ian's raised eyebrow and added, "Believe me, you need it."

Part of the reason I wanted to be a foster parent was that we might be able to give a better life to a little boy just like Ian had been. A little boy in need of some kindness and consistency and love to thrive. We could give that. There was a framed photo of Ian on the mantelpiece at his aunt Mabel's house, a school photograph in which he looked so unhappy and vulnerable, in a little shirt and a scruffy school jumper, that when I first saw it all I wanted to do was hug the little Ian.

"You look so sad," I'd said, picking it up for a closer look.

"Probably went to school without any breakfast or any lunch money again, or any dinner the night before," Aunt Mabel had commented wryly. I'd thought at first she was joking, but I caught a look between her and Ian and realized she wasn't. I'd never asked her anything more about his childhood, as I didn't want to have secrets from Ian and trusted that he'd tell me what he wanted to or what was necessary, but there were huge gaps in his past that he simply wouldn't—or couldn't—fill in.

*

"We'd like to do some nice things while the child's with us," said Ian to John, munching on some salad. "Take them on trips, holidays to the seaside . . ."

We'd loved seeing Emma and Freddy play in the sea and the sand, although Freddy found it almost impossible, despite repeated tellings-off, not to drink the salty sea water.

The professional foster parents' eyes widened in horror at Ian's holiday idea.

"They'll be worse than ever if you take them on holiday," said John. "They need to have a regular routine to feel safe and secure."

"Breaking the routine will only lead to tears and tantrums," added Nora.

I could see what they meant. The puppies liked to have a routine so they knew what was going to happen when, and on which day, but they didn't get all disruptive if the routine was temporarily changed.

"They're not little innocent Snow Whites, you know," Nora said. "They have all sorts of emotional and physical scars that you'll never get to the bottom of, or heal completely, and it comes out as lying, cheating and stealing. They try to break you down."

When it was time for them to leave, we saw them to the door.

"Len said you were helping to raise puppies for Helper Dogs," John said.

"We are," I smiled.

"Don't leave the foster kid alone with the puppy—ever," Nora said.

"But . . ." I'd thought a child would love having a puppy.

"One of the foster kids from the agency got hold of some matches, and fur . . . well, it burns, and a little puppy . . ."

I felt sick as I washed the pans and loaded the dishwasher. A little puppy was so vulnerable. How could anyone, however badly they'd been treated themselves, knowingly hurt one?

It had been a disappointing dinner with Nora and John. They'd seemed very negative to us, but perhaps after a while that was how you became. We'd thought we could become short-stay foster parents, looking after a child for a week or so if their parents had to leave home for some reason. We'd thought we'd be able to make their forced break from home a special experience, leaving happy memories. It sounded as if we were wrong.

Nevertheless, I was still looking forward to meeting Kirsty from Parenting Partners. As soon as I saw her beaming smile I thought, *At last!* Finally I'd met someone in the fostering and adoption world who was a little more upbeat. She even liked dogs.

We chatted all afternoon, talking about our experiences and what our hopes were. Kirsty told us that the agency usually dealt with children who were difficult to place, but if we were willing to take a child with special needs then she'd love to add us to their books. Then she turned to Ian and said she understood that he'd been taken into foster care himself when he was a baby.

"Yes, twice," he said. "Once when I was a baby and at least once when I was older."

"So that's more than twice, was it?" said Kirsty, a little puzzled. "What was it for?"

"I'm . . . I don't know . . . I can't really say. I don't remember very much."

Ian had shut down, and although Kirsty gently pressed him for details, she quickly hit a barrier.

Freddy padded in, and Ian took the opportunity to supervise Freddy outside while he did his business in the garden.

Kirsty whispered to me: "Meg, I'm worried about Ian. Children don't get removed from their homes without a very good reason and he's blanking it all out. He's such a lovely, gentle, kind man, but it worries me."

I nodded; I felt exactly the same. I knew Ian so well that I could tell what he'd be OK with, and what he wouldn't, and it felt to me that raking up bad memories would definitely not be OK.

"Everyone we take on as a prospective foster parent has to go through a detailed psychiatric assessment," she continued, "which involves a lot of digging into their childhood. Even just from this afternoon, I'm not sure, I'm really not sure, if Ian's ready to go back into his past. The assessment is hard enough for people who had reasonably good home lives, but for someone who hasn't . . . I don't know how much distress you want him to go through . . ."

Ian came back in with Freddy and Kirsty smoothly changed the subject.

I loved Ian for his sunny outlook despite the odds that had been so stacked against him, and also his generous desire to help people who were going through the sort of things he'd been through. When he was little, he sometimes used to help his uncle, a milkman, out on his round, he once told me, and one stop on the route was a children's home.

"The kids there always looked so happy and clean and cared for," he'd said. "I used to feel jealous of them. I wished I could stay there."

Yet despite repeated visits from social workers and the police he had only been removed from home for a brief time. I wanted to raise children with him in any way possible, and to help kids, but if I was forced to choose between his happiness and others'—even mine—well, there was no choice.

After Kirsty had left I poured us both a glass of wine and told Ian what she had said.

"It's going to mean you have to dig it all up and lay it all bare, and if you'd rather not, then we don't have to continue," I said. "I wouldn't want a happy family but an unhappy Ian."

Ian looked at me and looked at Freddy, and then seemed to disappear inside himself, as if the answer might be written on the walls he'd built inside his head.

"Truthfully, if that's what it's going to take, I'd rather not," he finally said.

That evening, Ian was sitting at the computer and I was looking through my diary. We were trying to make sense of it all. Freddy, fostering, dogs and children, but most of all us. It had been so long since we'd thought about ourselves.

The date was set for Freddy to leave, and after that we'd have a few empty weeks, a gap in our lives, before Traffy was old enough to leave her mum; we still had the money we'd been planning to use for IVF, and we both felt as if we needed a holiday.

"Fancy a trip to New Zealand?" said Ian, who'd never been there in his life. Prior to getting married I'd spent a lot of time there and had made some good friends who I knew would love a visit. Ian was browsing on a travel website: we could afford the trip, with a lot to spare. It was booked before we went to bed.

Having a holiday to look forward to and old friends to contact took my mind off Freddy leaving, but only a little. As with Emma, I took him to all his favorite places and played his favorite games, and though I couldn't say it was any easier, at least this time around I knew what was to come. I was also on the phone to Rachel every day to chat about the arrangements; if he was going to be staying with anyone, I was pleased that it was going to be Rachel, and she said over and over again we were more than welcome to visit him—every day if we wanted.

Time passed quickly, as preparations accelerated for Freddy's holiday (which is how I was thinking about it) and also for ours. Then, a few days before we left, a letter came from the council, which I thought would be about tax or something similar. I opened it: it was from the fostering and adoption service. I'd forgotten about them completely, felt they'd forgotten about us too, but now they were saying that they'd decided it would be OK for us to foster a child—just one. With the covering letter there were countless forms to fill in to begin the application process.

I made a mental note to tell Ian about it later but put it straight in the recycling bin. I had more important things to do.

Half an hour later I was at Marion's and feasting my eyes on little Traffy and her brothers and sisters. All the puppies' eyes were now open, and though she'd grown a lot since I'd last seen her, she was by far the smallest of her litter. But certainly not the quietest! She was a bossy, tiny little thing who told her brothers and sisters off with her tiny puppy-girl yap and chased after them as they ran after the empty plastic water bottles and beakers they'd been given to play with.

"Much cheaper than real toys and just as much fun," Marion's husband said.

I smiled and didn't mention Freddy's vast collection of "real" toys, or the zoo of stuffed animals that Traffy would soon own when she became ours.

I told Marion about our trip to New Zealand, and that we'd be back ten days before Christmas.

"I think little Traffy might be ready to come to you by then," Marion said. "I usually don't let them leave until they're eight weeks old, but I think I can make an exception of seven-and-a-half weeks for you, so you can have her for Christmas."

She'd be with us for Christmas. Our own, forever, Christmas puppy. Our first puppy who would never ever have to leave us.

I picked Traffy up and gave her a cuddle. "Maybe we should call you Holly," I said. But I knew Ian had his heart set on Traffy.

All our bags were packed the morning before we were due to set off for New Zealand. So were Freddy's. I'd spent the day before gathering together all his toys, vacuuming his doggy bed, and making sure he had at least a six-month supply of his favorite treats. He could see something was up, but he seemed calm—much calmer than I was. In truth, I was keeping myself busy, thinking of the holiday, of Traffy, even the terribly long plane journey—anything not to think about Freddy leaving us. Even so, every now and then a tear would slip out, and I'd lock myself in the bathroom to make sure Freddy didn't see I was unhappy.

That afternoon, Freddy didn't seem to mind a bit getting into the car with all of his stuff, and Ian drove us up to Rachel's. Rachel gave me a big hug when I arrived and quickly took all of Freddy's things away. Freddy, meanwhile, accepted a slice of salami from her, then leaped out of the car and proceeded to lap the garden at top speed four times, rolling, tumbling and barking with Gandalf, who had grown a little bigger than when I'd last seen him, but definitely no wiser.

"We shouldn't hang around," said Ian, knowing that the longer it took the harder it would be. I called Freddy over and said my goodbyes, whispering into his ear how much I loved him and was proud of him, and how even a forever puppy could never take his place. Ian said goodbye too, then we stood up to thank Rachel.

"Don't worry, he'll be fine," she said.

We drove away, and I watched Freddy playing with Gandalf on the lawn in the rearview mirror. He didn't even see us leave.

FRIDAY: GOODBYE

Meg packed up all my toys and my chews this morning. I tried to help her by having a last chew on them and taking the toys out of the bags she'd put them in. Meg didn't mind. She kept cuddling me and telling me what a good boy I am. Then she looked in the fridge and took out some cheese and some of my favorite sausages and put them in a bag for me. I tried to tell her I could eat them straightaway (although I was a bit full up, really) but Meg said I had to wait and gave me another cuddle.

Then Ian came home and we went to Rachel's house. We went to see Gandalf—he's my new best friend. He and I like to play and play and play. We were having such a good time that Meg and Ian let me stay a bit longer—Meg said I was to be a very good boy for Rachel and a good friend to Dylan—I'm always good (nearly). I expect they'll be back to take me home soon.

We called Rachel from the airport before we boarded the plane.

"How is he?" I asked, full of worry.

"He's great—all he and Gandalf want to do is play."

"They'll settle down soon."

"I'm sure they will. Have a great time and don't worry about a thing," she said. "Lots of love to you both."

I hung up, turned my phone off and studied the safety demonstration as we taxied towards the runway, feeling equally excited and sad at the same time.

22

New Zealand was a complete change of scene. Three weeks of the open air, open roads, mountains and beaches—time and space like a brush to sweep the cobwebs from the corners of the mind. We hired a camper van in Auckland and traveled down to Papamoa and Rotorua, where we marveled at the mud pools and geysers and lounged in the thermal baths. The ferry between the North and South Island was smooth, and we drove on to Nelson and Kaiteriteri. We kayaked on the amazing turquoise blue sea, and saw the seals at Abel Tasman National Park, before falling asleep on the golden sandy beach.

It made all our recent turmoil seem so far away. And, really, it was: half a world away, in fact, and Ian and I were free from pills and treatments, writing and work, families and fostering, free to have fun and enjoy each other's company. Whole hours passed, with old friends or just motoring along, without thinking about any of my puppies, past or future. We did, however, send Traffy a postcard saying we were looking forward to welcoming her to our home soon. Freddy got a postcard to say we hoped he was being a good boy and enjoying living with Rachel and Gandalf, and Emma got one saying that we hadn't forgotten her and we trusted she was still being just as good a friend to Mike as when we last saw her.

I was still feeling guilty about Freddy, about how much

more I should have done with him while he was with us. If it hadn't been for trying for a baby and my hormones going crazy, he'd have gone on more walks, been to more classes, had more fun.

If it hadn't been for . . .

"Shhh," Ian said. "He had a good time when he was with us and you did everything you could for him."

"So did you," I said. "All that puppy showering and cleaning up after him."

"Ah, Mr. Pup-Pup," Ian smiled. He was still hoping that Freddy would be returned to us. It was impossible not to hope.

We visited my London ex-neighbors, Ryan and Polly, who'd come to New Zealand for a holiday and ended up emigrating. They'd decided when they were dating—it had been mostly Ryan's choice—that they wouldn't have kids. He'd realized with a previous girlfriend that he didn't ever want children, and the relationship hadn't lasted; then he'd got together with Polly, fallen completely in love and become trapped in a dilemma. He knew that she badly wanted children, but he realized he loved her too much not to tell her the truth. During the course of one long night they'd bared their souls, found that it wasn't such a big deal and now, five years down the line, they were happier than ever.

Ry and Polly looked suntanned, relaxed and happy. They'd made tons of friends in New Zealand, plus they were setting up their own business together.

Over a beer Polly told me their lives were so full she didn't know how they'd have been able to fit a child in even if they had wanted to, which they didn't.

We went to an open farm with them and Polly fell in love with a baby pig that kept following her.

"Can we get a pet, Ry?" she said, as she stroked the piglet.

Ryan pulled a face.

"I hear pigs can be house-trained," I told him.

Time we didn't spend with friends we simply relaxed on our own. The whole holiday was a complete chill out and we didn't argue once, except for one day when I'd had a slight prang in the camper van. I'd been upset, Ian had been a little bit cross and so he took over the driving, in a "For heaven's sake!" sort of mood. All was quiet until he drove into a closed drive-in and sliced off the very top of the van. We got out to inspect the damage: a long fiberglass splinter was sticking up at a jaunty angle.

"It looks as if someone's tried to open the camper like a tin of sardines!" I giggled.

"No, it looks like the feather in a cavalier's cap," gasped Ian.

All we could do was laugh and laugh. Luckily, it was insured, and when we returned the van the people at the hire place laughed too.

Every few days, Marion e-mailed to update us with information about how our forever puppy was growing and the things she got up to. The puppies were weighed each and every day to monitor their progress.

"She's still the smallest and noisiest one," Marion wrote, and sent a photo of them all looking adorably cute and mischievous.

*

When we got back to England, now dark, with Christmas decorations on the high streets being battered by drizzle, I felt relaxed and at peace for the first time in almost a year. We hadn't gone on holiday specifically to get away from our baby problems, and we hadn't tried to avoid talking about them either; we had simply not needed to say anything about it, and we came back with a better understanding of what we both wanted. Each other and our puppy. And the million and one other things that life had in store for us.

It was sad to come back to a house bereft of Freddy's presence. It felt very empty, though there were remnants of our time with him still around—a toy here under the sofa, a chew over there in the garden—that I found as we unpacked and settled back in. We were used to being greeted ecstatically, Freddy over the moon with happiness as soon as we walked in the door, as if each time he hadn't realized we were coming back. Now, though, we felt lonely. One of the benefits that Helper Dogs bring is simple companionship. Many disabled people feel isolated and lonely, but it's much more difficult to feel so if there's a dog around the house. It had surprised me to learn that many disabled people are taunted and bullied when they go out. One of the women we'd met at Emma's graduation, Sally, had told us how she used to be frightened by the kids from her estate every time she went out in her motorized wheelchair.

"One time they decided to use me like I was their goalpost as I tried to steer my wheelchair through them," she said. "Every time one of them hit the chair with the football, or even better, me, they cheered. It was awful."

Her Helper Dog, Ollie, licked her hand as if he knew the memory was hard for her. Sally smiled.

"If you want to have a Helper Dog, you have to have a garden and I so wanted to have a Helper Dog. I kept on and on at the council and finally I got moved to a different flat, off that awful estate. Now I enjoy being at home, as there's always company, and I also enjoy going out. If I see a group of teenagers coming towards me, I don't think they're up to no good—I expect them to ask me questions about Ollie. Everyone wants to know about him and he loves all the attention. Don't you?"

Ollie put his head on Sally's lap so she could stroke him more easily.

On our second day back, we tried to phone Rachel to see how Freddy was getting on, but there wasn't any reply. I left a message and then drifted back to sleep in a haze of jetlag. The next thing I remembered was being jolted out of a deep sleep by the phone ringing again.

"Meg, it's Jamie. How was the trip?"

I removed the hair from my mouth and told him all about it.

"You'll never guess what's happened and who I've got here with me."

Instantly I thought something was wrong.

"Freddy . . ." I said, panic rising.

"Yes, but don't worry!" said Jamie. "He's living with me now."

Gandalf and Freddy had been unable to stop playing, even at night, and were too much of a handful for Rachel. She'd had to walk them separately, which meant that she was walking for four hours a day, and, on top of that, they were so overtired that they were getting bad tempered—although not with each other. Reluctantly, she'd asked Jamie to re-home Freddy, but he hadn't settled there either, so eventually Jamie had taken him in.

"Shall we take him?" My spirits leapt. "Do you want us to have him back? Ian would be over the moon."

"No, no, no," Jamie said, "Helper Dogs would kill me if I did that. It definitely seems to me he's going to make the grade. Freddy is fine with me and Frank. And you won't believe this, but he and Queenie get on like a house on fire."

It was hard to believe, but if any dog could get on with Queenie then it would be Freddy. Time and again he had proved he could play with any dog; really, he could play for England. With his charm and bounciness he'd converted even the most awkward dogs into playmates—the two St. Bernards aside. There'd been a Dobermann called Elsa at his obedience classes, whose owner had held on to her protectively throughout the class. Elsa had seemed very nervous of the other dogs, but after the class, in the play area, where they'd gone to do their business, Freddy looked at Elsa, gave a puppy play bow and danced around her. At first Elsa just watched, then she suddenly gave a little bark to show that she wanted to play too. Elsa's owner was amazed.

"Elsa never plays with other dogs," she said. "She's been frightened of them ever since she was attacked when she was a puppy, but she likes your Freddy."

Jamie had spotted this good trait in Freddy. Now that Freddy was boarding with him, Jamie took him to all the training center classes and put his talent to good use.

"He's helping me to teach problem dogs how to interact properly with other dogs if they don't know how to do so," Jamie said. He sighed. "I wish I could keep him—he'd be a real help at my classes—but Head Office is going to take him shortly."

I think everyone who met and got to know Freddy fell in love with him. Freddy was really no trouble to anyone, but Jamie was being given the runaround by a new batch of puppies, which I met on my first visit back to the center.

"I'm not sure about these four," Jamie said, shaking his head at the impish, totally cute Labradors that had been donated to Helper Dogs. "They're the most stubborn, in-your-face puppies I've ever met." The puppies were stopping overnight with him and Frank on their way up to the new Scottish satellite center.

Sometimes dogs are too timid and nervous to make successful Helper Dogs, but these new puppies didn't have that problem. If anything, they were too hyperactive, willful and easily distracted—not good qualities for Helper Dogs, but, at least, traits they might grow out of as they matured.

I looked at the wriggling, seething balls of fur in the crate in the office.

"Oh, Jamie, they're just puppies!" I said as I picked up and cuddled the nearest one.

"I can't convince you to take one, can I? I'm sure the Scottish center wouldn't mind." Jamie smiled, in the vain hope that we'd acquiesce. "They're little scamps, the lot of them, and I'm worried that if we don't get the best puppy parents involved, they won't pass their tests." He sighed.

Flattery was a good tactic, but it wasn't going to work on me today. I was getting ready to pick up Traffy in the morning.

23

The next day, in the dark, chill December morning, Ian drove us over to Marion's, the convertible looking forlorn in the cold, its heater struggling to cope. I had the softest of soft small blankets to hold our puppy in on the way back.

Marion's three adult Golden Retrievers came to greet us at the door. The fourth generation, all eleven puppies, were beautiful, lively, funny and just adorable. Marion pointed to one of the boys.

"The people who were going to take him let me down at the last minute," she said. "So if you'd rather have a boy you'd be welcome to have him instead. He's got a fine head and could make a great show dog."

We didn't want a show dog or any other puppy. We wanted Traffy, who felt like she'd been ours since she was a week old. Of the two other girls, one was going to Marion's friend and the other she was keeping to show, and one day hoped to breed from—meaning that four generations would live under one roof.

I lifted Traffy into my arms and gave her a cuddle until she started to wriggle, and then I put her back into the square play area with her brothers and sisters.

Marion gave us a printed sheet about the feeds that Traffy needed. She'd already been microchipped, had her first course of injections and had been given a fancy pedigree name in case we changed our mind and decided to show her.

"You can't have the name Rosie because that's what I'm going to call my girl," Marion said. She had forgotten that Traffy had been named almost from birth.

Finally everything was done and it was time to take her home. I carried her out to the car and Ian held her while I sat down, then put her on my lap on the baby blanket. She looked very comfortable and didn't wriggle or cry at all on the way home.

"She's the best puppy for going in the car so far," Ian said as she closed her eyes for a doze.

Back at our house I carried Traffy past the Christmas tree and lights out to her toilet area, which we'd moved from down the end of the garden to under the tree closer to the house. Our experience with Emma and Freddy had taught us that, like it or not, many of the early deposits wouldn't make it that far, so it seemed foolish to fight nature.

The first day disappeared in a daze of love, playing and new discoveries for Traffy. Computer wires, steps, the TV remote, sofas, teddies and more—a whole world of new sights and scents to make up for the canine family she'd lost. We had a crate for her, but as Traffy was our puppy, and with memories of the trials and traumas of Freddy's first few nights, we weren't going to use it. Instead, I let Ian have the bed and I slept with her on the sofa. With very few whimpers and whines on her first night alone, she slept. I didn't. I was alert for any disturbance or movement or sound she made and every time I thought she might need to go to the toilet I carried her outside. She looked so lovely and so confident that night, only seven-and-a-half weeks old, walking up and down our extra-long corner sofa to find a more comfy spot to rest on, showing the new house who was boss, then coming back and crawling onto me for a cuddle.

The next day, I was dizzy with lack of sleep, but ecstatic. For the first time we had a puppy with whom I could fall totally and utterly in love without the fear that one day she would be taken away, so I let myself love her with all my heart and she loved me right back. Wherever I went she wanted to come, and I let her. While I was working on the computer she'd fall asleep on my lap, and when I was in the kitchen cooking, she'd be watching me from just a couple of feet away. Ian bought her a little stool so she could climb on and off the sofa by herself, and we quickly resigned ourselves to the fact that she'd be spoiled, but hoped that her good nature would mean that she didn't take advantage of us too much. We watched her as she avidly ate her food mixed with special milk for puppies, resurfacing with her tiny muzzle and whiskers covered in whiteness.

"She's so adorable," our friends said when they came to meet her. We were totally besotted.

With only a few days left before Christmas, I made lots of biscuits in the shapes of dogs, stars, Christmas trees and stockings to sell at the Helper Dogs annual Christmas fête. Homemade treats, and anything dog-related, always sold well. Traffy's nose twitched at the smell of them baking, but I couldn't let her have any yet—they'd make her little stomach sick.

"When you're a bit older, then you can have some," I said.

*

I drove over that afternoon with the biscuits still warm and Traffy safe in a small car harness on the passenger seat. I was only intending to drop the biscuits off, introduce Traffy to everyone and go home, but when I got to the fête there was a local TV news crew. Jamie surreptitiously passed me a tiny Helper Dogs coat. He'd sent the troublesome litter on to Scotland, and that left Traffy with a glorious photo opportunity.

"Put that on Traffy," he hissed. "We don't have any tiny puppies, and we need more puppy parents. Tell her to put on her best performance and make the TV viewers fall in love with her."

I slipped the tiny "Helper Dog in Training" coat on her and the reporter lifted her into her arms. Traffy gave the reporter one of what I already thought of as her trademark stares, a really good, intelligent look. The reporter was too busy doing a piece to camera to notice.

"I'm here at the Helper Dogs Christmas Fête surrounded by lots of adorable puppies like this one . . ."

Traffy was still staring at the lady, but her look seemed to have homed in on one particular facial area.

". . . details at the end of the program, as they're looking for more volunteer puppy parents . . ."

Traffy's little tongue came out, and she licked the reporter's nose as the reporter squealed and laughed.

"That's the take," said the cameraman, pleased that the puppy had played cute on cue and brought some Christmas cheer to the report.

The reporter spoke to Jamie and Frank, and then a few of us were interviewed about our experiences of being puppy parents. I spoke about how much we'd loved Emma and Freddy, and how hard it was to give them up.

"I'd never want to take Emma or Freddy away from their new lives and the very important work they're doing, but I'll welcome them back home when they retire, for walks by the river, cuddles on the sofa and an endless supply of homemade treats," I said.

We got back from the center thrilled at the coverage for Helper Dogs and excited to be on TV. I also thought how grateful I was that Traffy wasn't going anywhere. We could give her all our love knowing that she was staying with us.

Also just before Christmas was Freddy's last day with Jamie. He was being shuttled down to the Head Office with the other new recruits and initiated into advanced training. Jamie was incredulous at the sheer amount of stuff that Freddy owned.

"He can't take all those toys you gave him," he said. "They'll never believe it when they see how many he has."

"But he loves his toys, especially his pink unicorn."

"Well, maybe he can take that with him—but no more."

Poor Freddy. I'd brought him some of his favorite milky bone biscuits with me and as soon as he saw me he was standing up ready for a cuddle and nuzzled himself into me. I was pleased to see that Traffy could tell he was special to me. Of all the dogs at the center, he was the only one she paid any attention to, and she wanted to be with him all the time, and he in turn was very patient with her as she climbed all over him. Whenever he moved she trotted after him like a little shadow puppy. It was really cute to see.

I tried not to cry again as I said goodbye to Freddy,

though this moment seemed less cruel, as he'd been taken from us once already. The time we'd had with him again was a luxury, an unasked-for bonus. I felt almost ready to send him off for his new life.

Nevertheless, I must still have been a bit of a quiver as I almost forgot to mention to Jamie an important issue that I'd been meaning to raise for weeks.

"Oh, one more thing . . . Ian wanted me to talk to you. His work in the city, they have a big corporate social responsibility department and at the end of each year they allocate money to some of its employees' chosen charities," I explained. "Ian wanted to nominate you, but we have to know what you could do with the money. How much should we ask for?"

Jamie grinned widely. "Oh, right. I'll take money from the capitalists any day! Spread the wealth and all that." He grew serious as he pondered how much he could ask for without feeling cheeky. "Well, a hundred pounds would buy us a good number of leads and collars, maybe a few blankets . . . and then there's the food bills." His face dropped at the thought of the endless bills Helper Dogs faced.

So it was settled.

"A hundred pounds, why not?" said Ian, nominating Helper Dogs on the form he'd been issued and scribbling the figure in the box. "It can never hurt to ask, and we know it's a good cause."

He sealed the completed form in an envelope and took it with him to work the next morning, his last day in the office before his Christmas break.

*

On Christmas Eve we received a photo and some news about how Emma was getting on from Mike.

"Our partnership just goes from strength to strength, thanks to your efforts with her when she was a puppy," he wrote. "We have settled into a good routine both at work and at home. Emma is in tip-top shape, very lean and muscular. I sometimes think I have created a monster, though, and she is constantly demanding exercise!"

The photo showed her looking trim and happy. It had been so hard giving her up, but it was worth it to see her so well and so loved. She was definitely where she belonged.

"And you're definitely where you belong," I told Traffy, picking up her warm little body to give her a cuddle.

"Definitely, definitely, Lady Puppington," Ian said.

Traffy had decided that when she dropped a toy off the sofa she should bark at Ian, and he should pick it up for her from the floor while she looked on. The first few times he'd laughed and done it—and she'd earned her nickname because she was so demanding and aristocratic. Then we'd realized we might be turning our little girl into a monster, a lazy dog that wouldn't lift a paw for herself. This was too much, even for devoted puppy parents like us, so we started applying a little more of the Helper Dogs discipline we'd learnt. Now she had to use her little stool to get off the sofa and pick up her toys for herself. It had worked for their pups, and we were sure it would work for ours.

That evening, I looked at her playing on the floor, caught up in some of the tinsel that I, feeling especially festive this year, had strewn around the room. Ian had never liked Christmas, and until Emma came along, he'd spent it out of the country, skiing or by a pool—as far away from his family as he could afford to go. When Emma had arrived the previous year, he'd canceled the holiday he'd organized for us on the slopes without a word of protest. That Christmas had been fantastic, and this year would be even better.

"Finally, we've got something really worth staying at home for," he said.

I looked at the tree, the decorations, at Ian watching Christmas telly with Traffy, adorned with tinsel, worrying at his leg, and thought that there was nothing else I could want in the world.

24

I started Christmas morning by performing my now familiar Yuletide toilet supervision in the freezing 6 a.m. darkness. Traffy was delighted to be up and out as usual, snapping at the snow that had fallen overnight and snuffling around the transformed garden. Each day, Christmas or not, filled her with the wonder and joy of being alive. I remembered the Christmas before with Emma, and her being exactly the same, and I smiled at the memory. Puppies would always be puppies, but how different Ian and I were now. As soon as I could persuade Traffy in, I cleaned the muck off her paws, gave her a chew as a seasonal treat and took her upstairs with me, taking care to secure the guard at the top so she couldn't climb down again without my say so. Then I slipped back into the toasty bed next to Ian, placing Traffy on top of the duvet. She scrabbled around, made herself comfy in a hollow next to me, curled her tail around her nose and closed her eyes.

"We're not getting a puppy again next Christmas," I said. "I want a lie-in next year."

Ian grunted sleepily and smiled. For him, 6 a.m. was already a bit of a lie-in. I didn't feel he was taking my Christmas morning conversation seriously enough, so I planted my icy hands on his chest. That got his attention.

"Stop! Stop! That's enough," he said, opening his eyes. "We won't have to get a puppy next Christmas. We'll have this one—and the Christmas after, and the one after, and the one after . . ."

That was better. I settled back into the warmth and closed my eyes.

A few hours later, we were outside again, properly dressed this time, with our lively little furball, Princess Puppington. She was still excited about the snow and kept sticking out her little tongue to taste it.

In a bid to calm her—or did I mean us?—down, we'd helped her open one of her presents, a soft pink duck, and she'd brought that out with her. The duck was almost as big as her and had startled her with the quacking sound it made when she bit it in the right place. She'd jumped back a couple of steps and surveyed it warily, then, deciding to assert her authority, jumped back into the fray, trying to find the sweet spot that produced the sound and looking very pleased with herself when she did so. Soon, I thought, she'd be meeting real ducks down by the river, and she'd be just as interested in them as she was in her toy one.

Ian got busy making the Christmas dinner and was in such a good mood he even let me put a CD of carols on. Last year it had been just the two of us and Emma; this year we were expecting my parents, my brother Jack, his partner Carmel and their little Maisie. Mid-morning, they presented themselves at the door with armfuls of presents.

"Hello, hello," I said as I kissed them all. Ian shook hands with Jack and Dad and suffered my mum giving him a peck on the cheek, although he didn't look very comfortable.

Maisie looked completely different from when I'd seen her as a shriveled premature baby. Now she was a smiling, bonnie six-month-old. Jack and Carmel obviously totally adored her. Their miracle baby.

"At first we were always worrying about how fragile she was," Carmel said. "I used to have nightmares that she wouldn't wake up."

"And now she keeps us awake," Jack joked.

"You did bring her milk in, didn't you?" Carmel said.

"Course."

My mum and dad had visited them as often as they could during the early weeks when Maisie had first come home from the hospital. The midwife had visited often too, and within a few months Maisie was given the all clear.

Traffy was very interested in Maisie's toys, more so, even, than in the wrapping paper, as she could sense that everybody's attention was focused on them. Maisie smiled at Traffy and stretched her pudgy baby hands out to her and looked as if she'd like to play with Ducky in return. I smiled too. Maisie was gorgeous. We'd got her a yellow Labrador push-along toy, a child's walker with wheels and handles to hold on to. It was a little early, granted—at six months old she wasn't thinking about walking anywhere soon—but when I saw it I hadn't been able to resist. She'd have use for it soon, and in the meantime she could use it to help her balance and stand, and ride on while her proud dad pushed it around the room. It was also providing quite a distraction for Traffy, who was circling it with an air of circumspection on her face. On the plus side, it didn't bark back when she yapped at it, but on the minus side it was a fair bit bigger than her, and she wasn't at all sure about wheels instead of paws.

Ian emerged from the kitchen around 1 p.m. with the

most fantastic Christmas dinner, the first one he'd ever made, and we let Traffy have a tiny sliver of turkey to celebrate her first Christmas with us. It was all so fun and new for her. With Emma and Freddy we'd been very strict and always given them the dry dog food provided, but with Traffy being our own pup we felt we could be a little more lenient, as long as we remained aware of how sensitive her puppy stomach was. It was all so new for us too. It felt as if we had a home, a family, to bring together, something complete—ours and ours alone—that we could rely on and build upon for the years ahead. Traffy loved the turkey, and in the months to come we found that we liked making food for her—usually chicken and rice with a few vegetables, but never onions as they can be toxic for dogs—more than giving her prepared food. We knew we were spoiling her, and that regular dog food and treats should have been good enough, but with chicken and rice as her staple she never became overweight and grew strong and healthy, with tons of energy.

Our first family Christmas all together was a day of happiness and treasured memories. Maisie adored Traffy, and Traffy was just fascinated by her. My mum looked on approvingly from the sofa over a slice of Ian's homemade Christmas cake. "My two beautiful granddaughters," she said. Mum and Dad were to become huge fans of Traffy's too and were always ready to volunteer to look after her if we wanted to go away. They'd stay at our house and take Traffy for walks down by the river, marveling at all the wildlife they'd seen through their binoculars while Traffy waited patiently for them.

*

That night, after everyone had gone, we beached ourselves on the long red sofa and switched the TV on.

"That was the best family Christmas ever," Ian said, and I smiled.

"Good." I paused. "You know what? I don't want anything more than this. I don't want to try for a baby, and I definitely don't want to have IVF, and I don't want to foster."

The options, in their various ways, had caused so much heartache—and only promised future disappointments for me or anguish for Ian. I felt ready to leave them behind. I didn't regret for a minute trying each one and taking the path that had brought us to where we were, but now it was time to let go.

"I think you're right," said Ian, drawing me close to him. "We have all the family we need now. I've got everything I could possibly want."

I cleared up all the wrapping paper, the crackers and the party hats and, wrapping the turkey bones up tight to discourage foxes, put it all out in the dustbin, along with the vitamins and the minerals, the herbal supplements, the thermometers and the ovulation sticks, all the paraphernalia of pregnancy that had been supposed to help but finally hadn't made a difference.

It was dark outside. Ian put his arm around me while we watched Traffy, a tiny light shape in the white snow, as she barked and played with the glow-in-the-dark ball Ian's parents had bought for her.

"Next year we're taking her skiing with us," Ian said.

Ian had some time off between Christmas and the New Year, so we relaxed and got to know our new pup. Traffy, we found out, was similar to Emma and Freddy in lots of ways, but completely her own dog in others. For instance, when Jo brought her daughter's dog to visit a few weeks after Christmas, Traffy shared her chew with her, something I'd never seen a dog do before. Traffy chewed on it for a little while, then Lulu had a go at it, and then it'd be Traffy's turn again. She also tried to share her chews with Ian, which I didn't think was quite so nice, but he didn't seem to mind.

One day, she found a toilet roll and rolled it down the stairs, in completely unself-conscious imitation of the Andrex puppies, and in exactly the same way as Emma and Freddy had, making me wonder if this was actually innate, genetically programmed behavior in Labradors and Golden Retrievers. Fortunately for us, each of them only did it the once—role-playing or exercising the stereotype, perhaps. And, just like Emma and Freddy, she liked being allowed on the bed. With Traffy, however, we put a little stool next to it, to encourage her.

The one thing Traffy really didn't like was cows. One day in the New Year, after she'd had her injections, we were walking past a field of cows with Traffy strolling along happily off her lead in front of us. When the cows saw Traffy, they all came running over to her. Traffy looked around, and even though there was a fence between her and them, she must have felt as if she was being chased by giants. She gave a yelp and ran away as fast as she could, disappearing around the bend. We ran after her, to find a fork in the track: two possible paths for Traffy and no sign of her at all. I ran down one, Ian the other. He found her hiding in a tunnel.

"It's OK, Traffy, it's OK," I said, giving her a cuddle.

She wasn't very keen on cows from then on and would bark and bark and bark at the sight of them, whether it was the real thing or representations of them—like a life-sized sculpture outside a pottery we visited or even cow-shaped playthings on springs in a children's playground.

Perhaps we'd become inveterate dog trainers, but we started to teach Traffy simple Helper Dog tasks. First, Ian taught her to pull the light cord when it was time to go to sleep, then I started getting her to search for my keys. Her training wasn't as strict or as fast as Helper Dogs would have demanded, and for every one thing we trained her to do, we also allowed her an equal luxury. As soon as Ian got up in the morning, for example, Traffy would take his warm spot and fall fast asleep, often snoring. It became a routine: Traffy would wake us up in the morning, our own furry alarm clock, Ian would get out of bed and she'd get into it.

Freddy, meanwhile, was having mixed fortunes in his advanced training.

"I just don't think they know what to do with him," Jamie said, reporting back to us about a visit to Head Office during which he'd asked after Freddy.

"Oh, there he is now." One of the trainers had pointed out of the window. Freddy was outside, waiting at the boot of a hatchback. Two elderly ladies tottered up and opened the boot; Freddy placed his front paws on the edge, then one old lady took his back right leg, the other his back left one, and together, wobbling slightly under the weight, they lifted him into the car.

Freddy hadn't been able to stay at HQ's on-site kennels: he'd become hyperactive and barked all night, upsetting the other dogs, so Helper Dogs had arranged for him to stay with two elderly ladies who lived nearby. Unfortunately for them, he found them complete pushovers and very quickly had them doing everything for him

"I couldn't believe it," Jamie said. "He could have jumped into that car as easy as pie, but oh no, he had to make these poor old women lift him. Two of them! I don't know what's going to happen, I really don't. I can't imagine him having any incentive to pass when he can live the life of a spoiled king."

I smiled. I liked the idea of Freddy being spoiled.

"They also say that he understands every command, but he won't do it unless he's asked in a sweet, high tone of voice, which is really pissing the advanced trainers off," continued Jamie. "They say they have to mimic you before he does anything at all."

That made me smile even more.

A few weeks later, however, we heard that Freddy had been working temporarily with a woman with multiple sclerosis. Beverly had an extreme form of the condition, which had struck very fast and left her in a wheelchair with almost no hand movement and very little speech. She was very depressed and, when she went to Head Office for assessment, hardly lifted her head or made eye contact with anyone. The trainers weren't sure if they'd be able to place any dog with her at all, but then Freddy went over to her and nudged at her hand. At first she didn't respond, but Freddy was persistent. He wasn't going to give up on her even if she'd just about given up on herself.

The trainers decided to let Freddy and Beverly work a little together. Everybody was amazed that when Beverly gave Freddy a command he rushed to do whatever she asked immediately, even though her speech was so distorted as to be unrecognizable, and barely louder than a whisper.

"I don't believe it," the trainer who'd done the most work with Freddy told Beverly. "He's doing more for you than he ever does for me."

Beverly smiled faintly.

During the training week Freddy and Beverly went from strength to strength. Freddy hardly left her side and began to take on some of the tasks her carer previously performed. Because he was such a large dog, he was able to help her out of bed and into her wheelchair by pulling back the covers and tugging on a short rope she was holding to help her upright. Then he'd nudge her legs over the side of the bed and would have lifted her into her chair if he'd been able, but that was too much even for him; he could, however, run and find her slippers, place them on her chair and then pull a rug over her to keep her warm.

At the end of the assessment period Freddy went home with Beverly. The two old ladies cried as they waved their little prince off to the life of servitude he'd chosen.

On the e-mail after-care bulletin I read about how Freddy and Beverly were getting on: "Freddy goes into the adjacent garage to empty the washing machine and tumble drier . . ."

"Hmm, not like you, Traffy," I said to our little girl. It had been a bright morning and I'd been hanging some washing outside, but Traffy had decided to help it dry by running

past the flapping sheets and tugging, as if they were a toy. She looked so funny that I couldn't tell her off with any weight behind my words, and even took a photo of her in mid-pull for her blog.

A month later there was more news: "Freddy now raises the alarm from other rooms in the house. He also brings in bread from the milkman . . . great job! Very careful and does not break the plastic wrapper."

"That's not much like you either, is it?" I said to Traffy.

Traffy had just started to bring in the post and was always very excited when the postman came, but she sometimes stood on the letters so they weren't easy to pick up, or pulled at them with her teeth to try and get a hold, which, if you weren't quick, could mean shredded bills.

A week or so later, I was working in the office upstairs, and I heard her bark but ignored her as I was busy. All was quiet for a few minutes and then Traffy arrived at the office door with three untorn letters in her mouth.

"Good girl," I said. "What a good girl you are." I went to find her one of her current favorite chicken cake treats that I'd made that morning. Slowly but surely, she was learning.

25

It was almost April, and the Helper Dogs HQ lawn was scattered with crocuses, with daffodils pushing up at the edges. A few trees were struggling to bud in the unseasonably chilly breeze. We had been invited back to Hertfordshire for Freddy's graduation. It was a handsome affair. As he walked smartly into the mansion's grand hall with Beverly's husband, three grown-up daughters and son, Freddy looked like he'd lived with them his whole life. It was obvious they all doted on him.

Beverly's husband spoke for her when the family was called to the front, as Beverly didn't feel up to speaking to an audience.

"I work away from home a lot," he said, "and until Freddy came to live with us I traveled in constant fear that something would happen to Beverly while I was away. A year ago, she fell from her wheelchair taking washing out of the machine and lay helpless on the concrete floor of the garage for hours until, by pure chance, the postman realized something was wrong and called an ambulance." Tears slowly started to roll down his face. "She could have died, cold, alone and afraid, and I wouldn't have known a thing or been able to do anything about it. Now I know she has the best carer possible looking after her twenty-four hours a day." He looked at Freddy and the dog returned his gaze. "He takes the washing out for her now—

so that's never going to happen again—but I know that if she did fall out of her chair for any reason Freddy would get help. He'd get the phone to her or press one of the emergency buttons around the house. Now when I have to go away, I don't have the image of my wife lying on the ground with no one to help her. Now I know she's safe."

Freddy rolled onto his side nonchalantly and looked like he was ready to take a nap. I remembered how, as a very little boy, we'd taken him to a barbecue and he'd fallen asleep in the middle of it all, oblivious to the people moving around him and stepping over him.

After the ceremony I gave Beverly the photographic diary I'd made of the time that he'd spent with us.

"He really did love his toys," I told her.

Ian nudged me and I looked over to see Freddy very interested in a woman holding a trolley bag with a yellow stuffed toy dog peeking out of the top. As she walked past, Freddy stood up and padded after her. Then, when she stopped to talk to someone, Freddy nosed his way into the bag, which was just the right height, pulled the toy out and then returned to Beverly's side with it in his jaws.

Ian and I smiled at each other. We were glad he hadn't lost all of his puppyish traits. I told the trolley woman what he'd done.

"Oh, let him keep it—it can be a late Christmas present to him."

Beverly's husband nodded at Freddy and said: "He's our late Christmas present, the best present we could ever have. He makes our lives better in a million ways every day."

Ian squeezed my hand. We were so incredibly proud of Freddy and of our small part in his journey to become a Helper Dog. Our little boy all grown up and making such a difference.

Traffy, now six months old, more cream-colored than Freddy and more curly coated than Emma, had come to the ceremony with us and was basking in the glory of being a bit of a Helper Dogs star. Her TV appearance had pulled in several new puppy parent volunteers in our area, so she was very popular with the Helper Dogs hierarchy, and with Jamie in particular. As I was taking her to Frank's obedience classes and was close friends with so many connected with the center, everybody was aware of how clever and obedient she was. She loved all the attention at the ceremony and made a special effort to sit in her cutest "I'm a good girl" manner, straight and tall and gazing up at me.

She was doing her "good girl" sit when Angela, the head trainer at Helper Dogs, asked if I might be interested in selling Traffy to Helper Dogs. I told her I wouldn't sell Traffy for a million pounds. She was almost at the age at which, had she been a Helper Dog, she would have been taken away from us, and I was so glad she wasn't going anywhere.

"Maybe she could become a demonstration dog instead," suggested Jamie, slightly taken aback by the ferocity of my reply. Now that was a different kettle of fish entirely. A demonstration dog: the public face of the charity promoting its good work and raising much-needed funds. I'd be happy, working for Helper Dogs and spending time with my friends; Traffy would be happy, as it was all just a big game to her anyway.

"Where do I sign up?" I said.

Two weeks down the line, Traffy was wearing her "Helper Dog in Training" jacket (Jamie hadn't got any with "Demo Dog in Training" written on them yet) and we were strapping her into the car to take her to her first school visit, accompanying Jamie to one of the many demonstrations and talks he regularly gave; this particular one was at a school for children with special needs, which each year selected a charity to support. This year it was Helper Dogs' turn.

"You're going to see lots of children today," I told Traffy. She was busy shaking a snake toy.

*

238

Jamie was waiting outside the school for us with Dylan, now an experienced demonstration dog. The head teacher, a tall lady with glasses, came out to greet us.

"I'm Ms. Mitchell," she said as she led us inside. "The children are so excited." Traffy trotted down the corridor close beside me, taking it all in.

In the first class we visited, I took Traffy around the small circle of kids, letting each child say hello if they wanted to. Some were used to dogs and were adventurous; some weren't and were very timid. Tim, a ten-year-old in a wheelchair was used to them because his gran had a Yorkshire Terrier. He desperately wanted to stroke Traffy but couldn't reach her from his chair, so Traffy stood on her back legs and put her paws on the armrest of his chair so he could pet her. Martin didn't want to stroke her, but his eyes never left her, and I could see he was fascinated rather than frightened. One of the girls, Jess, put her face close to Traffy's and hummed into her soft fur. Traffy seemed to think this was just fine. Melanie was more tentative, her hand darting out to touch Traffy and then darting back again.

"It's OK," I said, and Melanie tried again, a little slower this time.

The two dogs were spoiled rotten in the staffroom at lunchtime. Everyone wanted a cuddle with Traffy, and she barely had time for a drink of water and a little nap prior to the afternoon assembly. The children's dining hall also doubled as the assembly hall, and once the lunchtime food, crockery, tables and chairs were cleared away, the caretaker rearranged the chairs into a rough semicircle.

Jamie, Dylan, Traffy and I had a little wander around the playground while everyone took their seats.

"It's going really well," Jamie said.

"I love meeting all the children," I told him. "And Traffy and Dylan are being so good."

"Don't speak too soon," said Jamie, as we went back into the hall.

"Today," said Ms Mitchell, "we have some very special visitors . . ."

Traffy stared out at the children. She looked particularly interested in a toy that one of the nursery children was shaking—a pink rag doll.

All the children knew what Traffy and Dylan were, of course; their responses ranged from "puppy," "dog," and "wow-wow," to a bark or a simple smile.

Jamie told everyone about all the good things that Helper Dogs did, then deliberately dropped his keys and asked Dylan to pick them up for him, please—which Dylan immediately did. He then lay down again while Jamie carried on talking. Then Jamie dropped a pen, but this time Dylan wasn't so obliging. After three or four tries, poor Jamie was forced to improvise.

"Umm . . . do you always do exactly what your mums and dads tell you?" he asked the children. They laughed, and more so when Dylan rolled onto his back in the hope of having his tummy rubbed.

Traffy was good as gold, sitting and lying on command, and doing the "puppy high five" that Ian had taught her. While she did, I told the children about all the things she might do when she was older, and all the people helped by Helper Dogs. By the end, she seemed to have become completely accustomed to all the noises, people and distractions of the school and, although she was very weary, behaved perfectly when the kids were invited to come and stroke her one final time. I asked her to wave goodbye to them—a new trick—then thanked the head teacher, said goodbye to Jamie and set off for home.

As I drove back, with Traffy asleep on the seat next to me, I thought about how pleased I'd been with the way she'd acted with the staff and children. It had been a long, long day, but it had really seemed like she had worn the Helper Dogs jacket with pride. I couldn't wait to go on more demonstrations with her, showing off her learning as she grew older and helping the charity get the public understanding, new parent recruits and money it needed. Most of all, though, I was looking forward to curling up on the sofa and telling Ian about it all, with Traffy beside us.

I was looking forward to walks with Traffy by the river in the early morning as the days got lighter, watching the mist lift and the kingfishers dart along the banks. And to holidays at the seaside, to splashing about in the surf; and looking forward to the mountains where the whole family could play in the snow. Not just this year but next year, and for years and years to come. Traffy wasn't going anywhere, neither were Ian and I. It made me so happy.

When we arrived back, Ian was home from work for the afternoon and was equipped with some very good news.

"Sit down, love," he said. "Remember the charity submission I did at work? Well, the lady running the scheme rang me on the internal phones a while back, saying that usually they gave out far higher sums than the hundred pounds we'd put down. So I . . . I didn't say anything, because I didn't want to get your hopes up. I added a few noughts on . . . and we got it!"

My legs felt wobbly even though I was on the sofa. Even Traffy looked surprised.

"How much?" I asked, barely able to contain myself. "How much did they give?"

"Ten thousand pounds!"

I almost fainted and grabbed at the phone to tell Jamie. His normally level voice broke and wavered with excitement—as close as he ever would get to fainting, I thought—and he put in a call straightaway to HQ. They said that £10,000 would be sufficient to take a puppy from birth right through to graduation . . . and would Ian do them the honor of naming it?

"What letter are you on now?" he asked over the speakerphone.

"M," came the reply.

"Mmmm . . . Minnie," said Ian, finally, after a lot of "Mmmmmming."

We said a fond goodbye, after giving Helper Dogs the scheme's contact details and extracting a promise of regular e-mail updates and an invite to as-yet-unborn Minnie's graduation. I sank back into the armchair, stunned and yet glad that Ian and I had been able to give something back to Helper Dogs. When we'd been saying goodbye to Emma and Freddy, it had felt as if the organization had only been taking away from us, cruelly snatching the most precious thing in our lives, but now I realized that they'd given so much more. They'd given us two little dogs to love and care for, and through them a whole network of friends, trainers, puppy parents and disabled doggy partners who'd become almost like family. Most of all, without Helper Dogs, we wouldn't have ever met Traffy, who'd made our home complete. I glanced down at her, chewing on her rattlesnake in the doorway to the kitchen, then looked over at Ian, who looked as dazed as I felt, and smiled.

"Right," I said. "I think I'd like a glass of wine after all that."

"Let's toast the day," agreed Ian.

I lifted myself out of the chair and was walking toward the kitchen when the phone rang.

"Oh, hi there, Meg, it's Sarah from Baby Makers," said the voice at the other end of the line.

Baby Makers was the charity that had given me support and advice when I was having difficulty becoming pregnant, and who'd conducted the expensive hair analysis about which Ian had been so dubious. Looking back, I reflected, I wasn't surprised the hair analysis hadn't helped. But that was all over a year ago now and so much had changed since.

"I was just wondering if you eventually had a little one?" Sarah asked.

I told her that we'd decided not to go down the private fertility route as our chances of conceiving were so slim, and that we'd looked into fostering and adoption and decided that wasn't for us.

"So now we've had three little ones. Puppies," I said. "Three in one year—and the last one's still with us. She came just before Christmas and is staying forever."

"Do you know my own dog's ears pricked up when you

started talking about puppies," said Sarah. "Now he's brought his ball over."

I laughed. "Any opportunity for a play!"

"You sound very happy," she said.

"I am," I replied. "I have my baby. My very own creamy-colored, furry baby. And she's perfect."

Acknowledgments

Huge thanks to the many people who inspired the pages of this book. I've changed some names and locations and, to avoid a cast of thousands, I've amalgamated some roles, but I hope everybody who played a part in this chapter of my life recognizes him or herself, and how grateful I am. Thanks also to the many dogs and puppies I met, making each day better with a simple wag of their tail.

On the writing side, I'd like to thank my agent, Jon Elek, who believed in *The Puppy Book* from when it was little more than a one-line query; Dan Bunyard of Michael Joseph for commissioning it; and Max Leonard: planner, personal editor and prose polisher extraordinaire, who made a seemingly impossibly tight deadline possible.

Finally, and most important, thanks to Emma, Freddy and Traffy for being such stars and to Ian for agreeing to me telling the story of one very special year . . .

If you are concerned about the health or welfare of a puppy, contact your local vet, the ASPCA or one of the other national dog charities, who will offer advice.

For anyone thinking of buying a puppy, please make sure it comes from a good home—one where you're able to meet the puppy and the rest of the litter and his or her mum, more than once, before taking it home. Too many puppies are born into the cruelty of puppy farms, especially at Christmas, and animal shelters are overflowing with unwanted pets.

As the old saying goes: "A dog is for life . . ."